THE WEALTH POWER OF PROPERTY

SYDNEY 2021

BRETT JOHNSON

THE REAL ESTATE ANALYST

Published by:

The Real Estate Analyst
PO Box 276
CHURCH POINT NSW 2105
AUSTRALIA
www.therealestateanalyst.com
ABN 263 589 27 595

A catalogue record for this book is available from the National Library of Australia

Author: Johnson, Brett
Title: The Wealth Power of Property - Sydney 2021
ISBN: 978-0-6450791-1-1
Subjects: Real estate investment - Australia
Real property - Australia

DISCLAIMER

The publishers, Brett Johnson The Real Estate Analyst, it's related businesses, and the authors make no representation and give no warranty as to the accuracy of the proceeding information and do not accept any responsibility for any errors or omissions from the information contained herein (whether negligent or otherwise) and Brett Johnson The Real Estate Analyst shall not be liable for any damage howsoever arising from acting or refraining from acting in reliance on any information contained herein.

No reader shall rely solely on the information contained in this publication as it does not purport to be comprehensive or to render specific advice. Any reader should consider their personal circumstances when assessing the suitability of investment property.

Much of the information contained in this book is supplied by third parties believed to be reliable, however readers should make independent enquiries to confirm relevant details, as well as consult their professional advisers. This disclaimer does not purport to exclude any warranties implied by law which may not be lawfully excluded.

THE WEALTH POWER OF PROPERTY

SYDNEY 2021

BRETT JOHNSON

THE REAL ESTATE ANALYST

TABLE OF CONTENTS

BACKGROUND

For almost 30 years Brett Johnson and his father Fred Johnson jointly owned and managed Quartile Property Network, a property investment consulting practice based in Sydney, Australia.

Quartile's primary focus included monitoring residential property markets, advising thousands of private investor clients, and managing residential property for investors throughout Australia.

BRETT JOHNSON

Brett Johnson joined the family business of D.F. Johnson in 1982, specializing in property investment and portfolio management for institutions, corporations, and individual investors.

He has appeared on numerous television and radio programs and has delivered hundreds of presentations on property investment throughout Australia and New Zealand, advising thousands of people on property investment and property markets. He is an advocate of planned, counter-cyclical property investment.

FRED JOHNSON

Fred Johnson is the co-founder, together with his late brother Don, of the original D.F. Johnson property investment business which commenced in 1953.

He has authored and co-authored seven books on real estate investment including the best-selling "How to Get Real Estate Rich", "Riches from Real Estate" and the original "Wealth Power of Property".

His knowledge of real estate investment techniques and marketing strategies makes him one of Australia's leading authorities on residential real estate. He has toured Australia, New Zealand and the United States presenting his proven techniques of wealth creation through property.

FOREWORD

The original edition of The Wealth Power of Property was published in 1997, almost twenty-five years ago. It was co-authored with my father Fred who had previously written multiple books on property investment including the first one ever written and published in Australia.

In creating this edition, I have tried to retain the tone of the original text while being conscious of updating the data and in some cases the language while creating an edition based exclusively on the Sydney residential property market.

A significant difference from the original text is that we are no longer in the property consultation business. We are in the privileged position of looking back at decades of experience. In doing so I found a renewed freedom in speaking about the market and the investment process.

There are many tips and insights throughout these pages. The things we have learned over the years which we are delighted to pass on to you. Hopefully, it will prove to be a turning point in reaching your financial objectives or securing a better lifestyle.

On a housekeeping note, we have used examples of property growth rates and rental returns throughout this edition. All data and time periods are rounded and used for illustrative purposes. Where an inflation rate is discussed we have used the rate for Australia.

Thank you for acquiring the Sydney 2021 edition of The Wealth Power of Property. We hope it helps get you to wherever it is you want to go.

Cheers

Brett Johnson
The Real Estate Analyst
Sydney 2021

Chapter 1

WHY RESIDENTIAL PROPERTY?

"We must be getting close to Sydney; they're talking about real estate on the radio".

This book sets out to provide you with a detailed explanation of the benefits of residential property, and its wealth accumulation prospects, in an easy-to-understand way, using the Sydney residential market as the context for discussion.

If the correct principles are applied, it is possible that anyone can achieve property wealth. We know of no other way to methodically plan exceptional asset accumulation with reasonable safety and certainty, aided by tax advantages, leverage and historically consistent capital growth, as that available through residential property, above all other investment mediums.

Residential property has a long and successful history of investment performance with minimal risk. One of its outstanding features is long term capital growth, or the potential for increasing property value over time. It is this factor that allows us to build growth into our net worth while the rental income allows us to service the investment and provides the means to own more.

Historically, we can learn a lot. In 1965 the median three-bedroom house price in Sydney was $11,800. In 2020, fifty-five years later, it was $1,103,100.

Through that entire period, people and publications have been telling us property is not a good investment.

Back in the early sixties we had the "Menzies' credit squeeze" as it was called. Credit dried up. It was a difficult time.

"When money is tight, people cannot afford to buy, values cannot rise".

Then through the late sixties and early seventies came a share boom and bust. By the mid-seventies we had political turmoil and another recession. In the late seventies we saw rising inflation and the OPEC Oil crisis. The early eighties brought another severe recession, then boom, then share crash.

SYDNEY HOUSE PRICES (Three bedroom single dwelling)
June Quarter Median

Year	Price	Year	Price
1965	$11,800	1993	$180,000
1966	$12,600	1994	$194,000
1967	$13,400	1995	$213,000
1968	$14,800	1996	$220,000
1969	$16,200	1997	$241,000
1970	$18,500	1998	$272,000
1971	$20,600	1999	$296,000
1972	$23,700	2000	$337,000
1973	$26,400	2001	$364,000
1974	$33,000	2002	$452,000
1975	$33,800	2003	$519,000
1976	$37,300	2004	$552,000
1977	$39,400	2005	$528,000
1978	$45,800	2006	$525,000
1979	$54,800	2007	$525,500
1980	$69,700	2008	$542,000
1981	$84,700	2009	$544,000
1982	$84,300	2010	$624,000
1983	$82,900	2011	$644,700
1984	$84,500	2012	$642,400
1985	$92,200	2013	$690,100
1986	$104,600	2014	$811,800
1987	$122,800	2015	$1,004,800
1988	$171,000	2016	$1,023,192
1989	$210,000	2017	$1,194,200
1990	$175,000	2018	$1,130,300
1991	$186,000	2019	$1,020,700
1992	$176,000	2020	$1,103,100

Source: REIA, ABS, BIS Shrapnel

There was always a reason why we should not invest in property.

We had a major boom in values in Sydney from 1986 to 1989. Prices doubled over a three-year period.

"Our children will never be able to afford property".

"Prices will never go any higher".

The early nineties featured another recession followed by falling inflation. Since then, we have had various economic shocks from dot.com busts to the GFC, but had managed to stay out of recession, until the pandemic. Today we have a weakened economy with challenges ahead, but remain in a stable, low inflation environment a bit like the mid-sixties.

During that fifty-five years, values increased from $11,800 in 1965 to $1,103,100 in 2020, a rise of 9,348%, or 8.6% per annum compound.

If you measure to the most recent peak in Sydney prices being $1,194,200 in 2017, the compound growth rate since 1965 is 9.31% per annum.

It used to be a cliché that house prices increased at around 10% per annum. During that fifty-odd year period, it has been almost true. But that does not mean it always will be.

There is a critical relationship between price growth and the rate of inflation which we will explore in a later chapter. For now, the point is the power of growth upon growth and how to use it.

THE POWER OF COMPOUND GROWTH

It is the compounding effect of property values over time which is so powerful. As each year passes, growth occurs on growth.

In round numbers, if a property is worth $100,000 and increases in a year to $110,000, it has increased by $10,000 or 10%. The following year it also increases by 10% from $110,000 to $121,000 an increase of $11,000.

Growth is accelerating at a faster rate as each year passes. By year ten that property would be worth almost $260,000. After 20 years it would be worth $672,750.

To use a well-worn gardening analogy, it is a bit like planting a tree. Early growth is slow, but as it establishes it grows faster, and starts to bear fruit. The fruit drops, and more trees grow and start bearing fruit.

Before we know it, we have an orchard. It is a similar compounding effect with property.

Property wealth comes ever so slowly at first, but eventually it does. All you need is time, information, and patience. These are the main ingredients.

The goal is to use compound growth, and the qualities of time, information, and patience, to our advantage, in the safest possible way, to improve our lifestyle, and to achieve independent financial wealth.

So why residential property in preference to other types of property?

HOW SAFE IS RESIDENTIAL PROPERTY?

Let us analyse the residential property market and see why we believe it is the safest, and most profitable market in Australia.

The total value of all residential dwellings in this country is around $6,800 billion. That is, about three times the size of the share market, almost eight times the size of the commercial property market, and at least 25% larger again than all other major investment markets combined, including super funds and banks.

It is not special just because it is big. But it does have some interesting attributes.

In Australia 65.5% of the residential market is made up of owner occupiers, that is people living in, owning, or paying off their own homes. It has come down a bit in the last 20 years after hovering around 70% for almost 50 years.

Overall, the level of home ownership in Sydney and across Australia has remained relatively consistent despite property cycles and despite economic booms and recessions albeit with a more recent downward trend.

OWNER OCCUPIERS - THE SAFETY VALVE

That level of home ownership is the main reason for the security, reliability, and predictability of residential property as an investment.

Owners occupiers, people who own their own homes, do not panic and rush to sell en masse when times get tough as investors sometimes do in other sectors, especially the share market. This provides a built-in safety net for the residential property market.

Residential property is the only investment market that is not dominated by investors. It forms a defence against substantial downside in the marketplace. It is a unique feature of residential property as an investment commodity.

Everybody must be housed, whether they rent, or owner occupy. The low volatility of residential property values is underpinned by owner occupiers who do not sell if a market lacks strength. They need more compelling reasons.

Maintaining good occupancy is important to the successful outcome of a property investment. Around 30% of Australians rent where they live, providing a huge pool of around 7.5 million Australians who require rental accommodation.

Rental markets fluctuate over time of course but it is never all that difficult to find a residential tenant – if you are prepared to meet the market.

IS VACANCY A PROBLEM?

Over the long term, residential vacancy factors tend to fluctuate between 0.5% and 6%. The larger being the worst-case scenario. It would rarely be worse, but is a risk that can, if necessary, be built into the investment feasibility.

Alternatively, because that large pool of prospective tenants exists, a reduction in rent can negate the vacancy factor. There may be times when that is necessary. Either way it can be budgeted and managed. Periods of prolonged vacancy in residential investment are unlikely where good management and property maintenance are provided.

This is not necessarily the case with other types of property. Driven by economic considerations, factories, offices, and retail property cannot promise the same continuity of income. Their occupancy depends not on the need for shelter, but the expansion of business and growth in the economy. This can be critical where borrowed funds need to be serviced out of income and a long vacancy persists due to economic contraction.

Other growth investments such as shares carry similar risks, as the continuity of dividends depends on profitability and business expansion. The pandemic has clearly demonstrated the impact of this with banks reducing or suspending payments of dividends.

In our opinion, these factors put residential property on the top shelf of investments. The 65.5% of the population who are homeowners provide a solid base to values, minimising volatility in the market, while the 30% who rent ensure a large dynamic market for the maintenance of income.

A TANGIBLE ASSET

Another feature of residential property which is important, is that you own it in your own right. It is a tangible asset. You own it directly. You monitor its performance. It is totally under your control. Other than perhaps having a good property manager you do not need to retain a conglomerate of advisors speaking investor-babble to help you manage it.

You can use that ownership to your advantage by leveraging your ability to own more property and attract more growth.

Chapter 2

WHY DO PROPERTY VALUES RISE?

MEASURING PROPERTY VALUES

We have talked about the long-term growth in residential values but what makes a market sometimes rise, sometimes fall, and other times simply move sideways or do nothing? In the Sydney Residential Prices Chart we can see the movement of house prices in Sydney from 1965 to 2020.

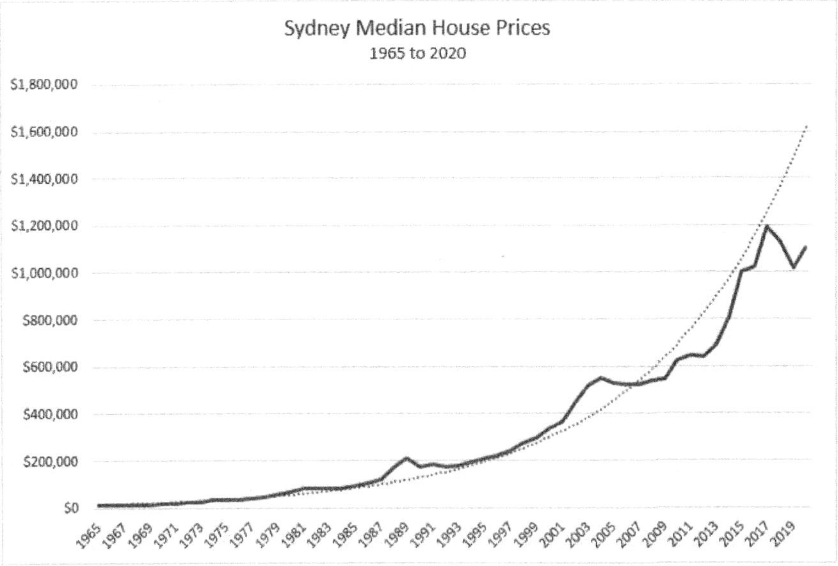

These are nominal house prices. The same figures we saw in the previous chapter and which we are used to reading in property reports and in the media.

The broken line is the exponential trend line which smooths the long-term growth rate and reveals periods of an over-valued and under-valued market as prices snake their cyclical way around the longer-term trend.

Removing the effect of inflation on nominal price changes reveals even more.

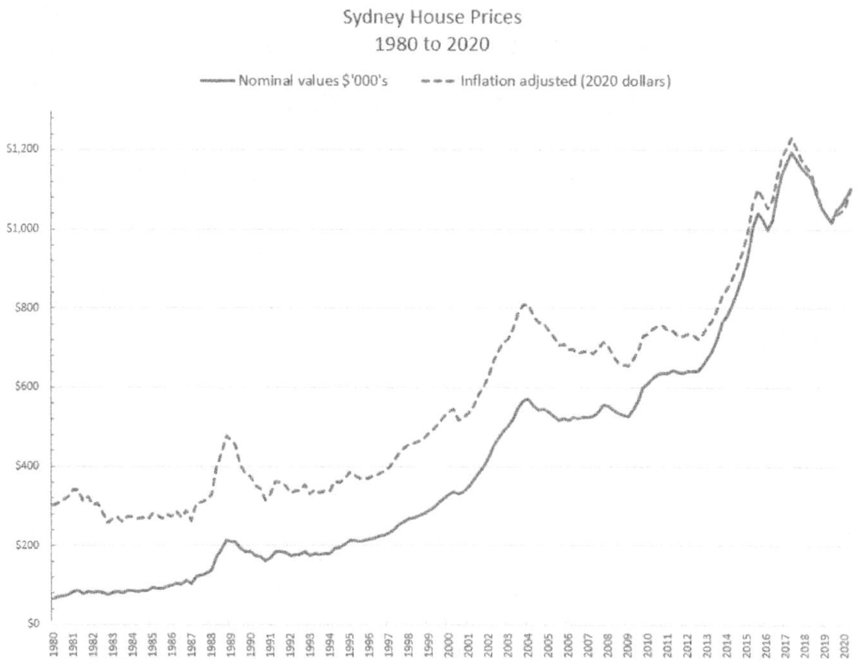

In this chart we can see nominal prices in the solid line and inflation-adjusted values (in 2020 dollars) in the broken line.

We do this for two reasons. The first is, the movement of the value of any capital asset, in this case property, above or below the rate of inflation is important because we want to know how values have changed in relation to the actual cost of living.

If you buy a property today for $100,000 and, in ten years it is worth $200,000, but everything else is also twice as expensive, then you have not achieved much at all. You cannot do any more with your money despite your property doubling in value.

It is the growth in values above the inflation rate that delivers the real benefit. That is where it really counts.

The second reason is that when you deduct the inflation rate, it accentuates the real market cycle. You can see in the chart a clear cycle fluctuating over time. We can also see that at various times, values are rising strongly above inflation, and other times values are falling significantly in real terms. In nominal terms they may be rising or levelling off while in real terms they may be declining.

HOW PROPERTY CYCLES DEVELOP

"Why do values rise at certain times and fall at others?"

During a period of very strongly rising values, several things happen. Most notably, the rate of construction of new property increases. The reason this happens is that developers and speculators are constantly out in the market watching the investment and development feasibility equation. They are monitoring land costs, calculating that if they buy land for X, expend Y on construction and then sell for Z on completion, the difference of course is the profit margin.

When values are rising strongly prospective profit margins are significantly enhanced. When there is a greater potential return, more will commit to development, therefore the rate of construction increases, sometimes dramatically.

Nobody tells builders, developers, or speculators when to stop. They keep building as values are rising, to take advantage of the strong market. Eventually more dwellings will be built, and placed in the market, than there are people to occupy them.

When there is a surplus of property and not enough people in the market to buy them, or rent them, the market will stall. Values tend to ease then level off, and with inflation at work, as you can see in the chart, real values may continue to decline. Developers, and speculators then withdraw from the market and the rate of new construction will decline. This can take time, as it is not easy to withdraw from the market if buildings have been commenced, so the construction level continues to overshoot for some time.

Despite the softness in prices at that time, the population continues to increase, and those reaching household formation age or arriving as immigrants from overseas or interstate continue to enter the market. This slowly absorbs the excess construction of the previous boom.

ARE PROPERTY MARKETS PREDICTABLE?

One of the great things about residential property is we can see the market coming. We know the people who reach what the statisticians call household formation age, those born twenty-five to thirty years ago, are about to enter the market. We know how many of them there are, and we can predict their approximate time of arrival. It provides a comforting element of predictability.

As the excess construction starts to be absorbed by ongoing demand, the first signs start to appear in the rental market.

The vacancy rate, that is, the proportion of rental properties in the market that are vacant at any point in time, will start to fall as it reflects the tightening market. As a result, rents will start to rise. When rents start to rise yield-seeking investors are usually the first to sit-up and take notice. If values remain relatively flat, and rents rise, then the prospective income return, or rental yield, an investor may receive increases, attracting them back to the market.

As investors re-enter the market after a downturn, the market will start pushing prices up slowly. Home buyers see values rising. These people, especially first home buyers, are very price sensitive. If values increase, their required deposit also increases. Many of us remember the problem, constantly striving to save the deposit only to see it slip from grasp as values are pushed up higher. But that attracts more buyers, including growth-seeking investors, creating a snowball effect, setting off the next price upturn. Construction increases as the developers become active again, projecting us into the next cycle.

THE SUPPLY AND DEMAND EQUATION

The supply and demand pendulum will swing back and forth forever. We can see it clearly at work in the chart with four cyclical peaks in the Sydney market over the last forty years.

There have been many examples over the decades of periods where a major city market in Australia has been rising while others remain stagnant or in decline.

A good example is found back in the eighties in the way Sydney and Melbourne behaved so differently. Between 1980/81 and late 1985 the Sydney market was dead flat. Prices barely moved for five years. The market was over-supplied from the previous boom. That period also included the recession of 1982 and 1983 which affected the whole country.

In Melbourne, in December 1980 the median house price was $43,200. By June 1986, despite recession and other impacts, it had doubled to $87,000. The market was under-supplied and came out of the recession firing on all cylinders.

Of Australia's two largest cities, subject to all the same environmental and economic conditions at the time, one doubled in value, the other did almost nothing.

You can see the importance of supply and demand in determining whether values will rise or fall, overshadowing interest rates, tax changes, budgets, elections, and other forces. Supply and demand drives prices. Other factors can affect the timing of price changes, but supply and demand are the fundamentals in determining whether values will rise or fall.

TYPES OF PROPERTY INVESTMENT

There are two types of property activity. Firstly, there is speculative real estate - real estate bought for short term resale at a profit - sometimes called flipping.

Typically, an old house bought relatively cheaply, painted, maybe kitchen and bathrooms renovated with some outdoor tidying up and other cosmetics, in the hope that there is a reasonable profit when sold.

We do not know anybody who earns a consistent living out of doing that. It is a legitimate activity, but we should not call it investment. These people are in the business of trading property. It is even taxed differently.

Most of all, it is speculative, it is risky and should be avoided by most investors without special knowledge or experience. In times of strongly rising values some speculators do make profits from short term trading, but it is generally the result of an overall rising market at the time. It is mostly the land that is rising in value not the improvements.

The second type of property activity, is investment in income producing property, bought to maintain and hold for rental income and future capital growth. This approach we call investment. This approach builds wealth.

Chapter 3

PREDICTING PROPERTY MARKET GROWTH

THE SYDNEY RESIDENTIAL MARKET MODEL

One thing which stands Sydney apart from other urban areas and which will always contribute to the scarcity of serviced land in Sydney, is the geographic restrictions which contain Sydney into a finite area.

Unlike other cities in Australia, which tend to be flatter topographically, and have an ongoing supply of new land by servicing and subdivision, Sydney cannot easily continue to urban sprawl.

Sydney is surrounded by natural boundaries with national park and gorge country to the north, ocean to the east, national parks and water catchment areas to the south and the Blue Mountains and national parks to the west.

A FUNDAMENTAL APPROACH

The forces of supply and demand have always been the engine that drives residential prices. All things being equal, if demand exceeds supply, prices will rise. If supply exceeds demand, prices will fall, or remain the same. If demand equals supply, nothing much will change. But in property terms, what is supply and demand?

If we break down supply and demand into their various components, we can identify the likely direction of price movements at any point in time. This was the basis of a market model which we developed over many decades which became an indispensable tool for making investment decisions.

SUPPLY

Supply of property in a residential market means the total stock of dwellings which exist in that market. For example, in Sydney there are currently around 1.85 million residential properties.

Forecasting changes to the number of dwellings is the important point. This involves quantifying the likely rate of completion of new dwellings, the number of demolitions of existing dwellings, allowing for second or holiday homes which are not primary residences and for any rental vacancy factor.

DEMAND

Demand in a property market relates to the number of households which require a roof over their heads, and how that changes over time. Sounds simple, but in fact, is quite complex and strangely fascinating.

Consider the ingredients which make up residential property demand. It starts with a long list of shifting demographics from the shrinking size of households, increasing lifespans, the increase in single person households, high divorce rates, children living with parents longer, marrying later, having children later and the actual birth rate itself.

Add to this ant's nest of activity the immigration cycle, interstate migration, changes in employment locations and work practices, the impact of AI, the information revolution and shocks like a global pandemic and it is clearly a complex mass of swirling variables.

Yet these ingredients come together to tell us the rate of new household formation for a market, and therefore the number of dwellings that are required to house that population.

HOUSEHOLD FORMATION

We know over the last couple of decades the average household has shrunk from 3.6 people to 2.6 people today. You could rightly conclude that even if total population did not increase, this change alone has been generating increased demand for housing.

Falling household size is the result of many changes in the demographic make-up of our population. Longevity is an obvious factor. People are living longer. This has another impact on property, in that we are also healthier and more agile in retirement, causing us to remain in the family home longer than our forebears may have. A high and increasing divorce rate is also a major contributor to falling household size where one household separates to form two.

NATURAL INCREASE

We know the approximate rate of new household formation likely to occur from natural population increase, that is, ignoring immigration and other factors. This is because people do not form households when they are born. We form new households when we leave the parents' nest and this, on average, occurs when we are in our late teens or early twenties, although it has been getting later - especially during tough economic times. Therefore, we can predict how many households may form from this source in any period because we know how many people were born say twenty to twenty-five years ago.

INTERSTATE MIGRATION

It seems odd even talking about interstate migration when state borders are opening and closing with the pandemic. Nonetheless, people moving from one state to another is a real thing and sometimes in surprisingly large numbers. Some years ago, up to a net thirty-eight thousand people a year were leaving Sydney, in the majority for Queensland. In recent years this has reduced to a more typical thirteen to fifteen thousand a year.

Interstate migration is linked to the property price cycle. When Sydney prices are high, more people than usual take the opportunity to sell and move outside Sydney. Sydney has been a net loser in the interstate immigration stakes for many decades. Where Sydney wins a much larger share of the demand pie is in immigration. People coming to live in Australia.

IMMIGRATION

The interesting thing about immigration is the extent to which it is an obvious political football and the myths which surround the effect of immigration on the property market.

In the late 80's when prices in Sydney were rising strongly and immigration was at high levels, the conventional wisdom connected the dots and concluded the strong price rise was specifically caused by high immigration.

At its peak, immigration during that period increased from around one hundred thousand to one hundred & sixty thousand people per annum into Australia. The effect of that increase on the Sydney market is straight-forward.

Total additional people	60000
Around 30% settle in Sydney	18000
Number per household (at that time)	2.8
Number of additional dwellings required	6,428 per annum

That is a healthy boost to demand but when we put it in context, the Sydney market was already undersupplied after a six-year shortfall in new construction and required 27,900 additional dwellings per annum just to meet normal annual demand let alone catch up with the construction deficit. The result was a huge increase in house prices during that period which had been building up steam over several years. Immigration was a factor, as it always will be, but was not the specific cause.

Extraordinary demand from any source does not necessarily lead into a strong market. The level of demand must be weighed against the ability of the market to supply the dwellings to meet the demand.

For a long time, Queensland experienced huge population growth, gaining the largest share of interstate migration within Australia and an increasing share of immigration into the country. The building industry in that state still managed to produce so many new dwellings that supply well and truly exceeded even incredibly strong demand leading to a soft market, high vacancy rates in the rental market and areas of falling values.

It is the balance between supply and demand which determines the result.

BALANCE

All the factors which make-up supply and demand can be brought together to create a picture which indicates the likely oversupply or deficiency of housing stock in the market.

Where under-supply is indicated, the natural conclusion can only be that given reasonable economic conditions, the growth engine is fuelled up and prices should rise.

Equally, if the market is oversupplied, even in strong economic conditions, the tank is empty and growth other than perhaps keeping up with inflation is less likely.

The best example of these forces at work is the comparison between the Sydney and Melbourne markets during the 1980's, which we previously discussed.

As we have seen the Sydney residential property market has a strong history of value growth over time, with a growth rate since 1965, including periods of low inflation, of around 9% per annum compound.

This is well above the rate of inflation, and when combined with rental returns, places residential property as one of the strongest performing investments available. It is also one of the safest forms of growth investment available, showing less volatility than other forms of investment.

THE CURRENT SYDNEY MARKET

Prices

Median house prices in Sydney last peaked in 2017 at $1,198,000. Values then eased to a low of $1,020,000 in 2019. By June 2020 house prices had recovered half that decline climbing to $1,103,000.

Prices remain below long-term trend however the pandemic may have taken the wind out of those sails for a while yet despite the more recent trend away from densely populated locations.

Vacancy Rates

The vacancy rate in the rental market is one of the leading and best indicators of what is really going on in the broader residential property market. A vacancy rate trending up indicates a market moving into oversupply while a vacancy rate trending down reflects a growing shortage of property.

If keeping track of demographics, construction levels and all the other factors we have been talking about is too much, then just keep an eye on the vacancy rate. It speaks volumes.

Having said that, vacancy rates in New South Wales are currently the strangest we have ever seen.

The highest vacancy rates in New South Wales are in inner and middle-distance Sydney suburbs at around 5% which is historically high. Remarkably high. But somewhat understandable given the impact the pandemic has had on work practices especially in higher density areas.

The vacancy rate in outer Sydney is around 2% which is a little under market equilibrium so not doing too badly. There was a mid-pandemic spike in July 2020 of 4.3% but that seems to have settled.

The Hunter and Illawarra areas have seen vacancy rates fall since the pandemic began and currently sit at around 1.5% and are continuing to trend down.

In every other region in New South Wales vacancy rates have fallen to historic lows. Except for New England and the Northern Rivers all regions in the state, as of November 2020 were below 1% vacant. Quite extraordinary.

Throughout the first year of the pandemic, it became obvious that people were actively taking the opportunity to decentralise as working from home became feasible. In many parts of the state that trend was well underway before the pandemic began with some regional locations starting to trend down when the Sydney market hit its price peak in 2017. That is when the exodus started, the pandemic has perhaps sped that phenomenon up.

What it means is there is a significant demographic shift going on and we need to be mindful of it in our overall assessment of markets and their prospects.

It does not mean we should all rush out to the country towns of New South Wales looking for our next investment. We remain unconvinced that smaller population centres present reasonable prospects for long-term capital growth.

Investor Activity

Investor activity in the Sydney market has been subdued since the cyclical peak in prices in 2017.

More recently, in October 2020, just over 23% of new residential loans nationally were made to investors, a significant increase over the previous few years.

Despite this, we would not expect to see a significant upturn in investor activity in the Sydney market until rental yields are attractive enough to compete with share dividends and outweigh any perceived risk.

Rental Yields

Gross rental yields, that is the gross annual rental divided by the property's purchase price or current value expressed as a percentage, are a measure of a property's ability to generate income. The net rental yield, that is, after all property related expenses are deducted, is more important when considering a specific property for purchase, but we will cover that later.

The gross rental yield provides a handy market indicator which tells us how the relationship between rents and values is behaving in the broader market.

Rental yields are usually at their highest just before a market moves into recovery and prices begin to rise.

As you might expect given recent rental vacancy rate changes, rents in inner Sydney have fallen dramatically in the last 12 months reducing by up to 25%. Across the Sydney metropolitan area rents have fallen anywhere from about 4% to 10% depending on specific location.

The difference from area to area is not a function of price bracket either. In the eastern suburbs rents have fallen around 20% while the northern beaches have seen rents rise around 5% for units and 15% for houses during the same period.

But as we said, the relationship between rents and values is one of the keys to understanding where a market sits in its slowly unfolding property cycle.

Being an important market indicator, we tend to monitor and rely on the gross yield for two-bedroom apartments as they are the most common property type in the rental market.

The median unit price in Sydney is currently $764,000. The median rent for a two-bedroom apartment has been falling since the market peaked in 2017 and is currently around $465 per week. This translates to a gross rental yield of 3.2% which is quite low in historical terms.

Keep in mind there is huge variation going on in different parts of Sydney in both prices and rents. We have recently seen gross rental yields of up to 4.6% in some parts of greater Sydney and at that level, against a background of low inflation and low interest rates it starts to get interesting.

Interest Rates

Interest rates are also at historic lows. The Reserve Bank has repeatedly stated, most recently on 1 December 2020, that interest rates are likely to remain at current levels for at least the next three years.

Over many decades the most common form of borrowing by residential property investors has been a three-year, fixed rate, interest only loan.

Of the four major banks in Australia, the current average rate for this type of loan is around 2.7%. This is less than the median gross rental return widely available across the Sydney market and significantly less than in some specific locations especially in outer suburbs.

SYDNEY MARKET FORECAST

If we ignore the influence of the pandemic on the Sydney market what we see is a market approaching four years since the last cyclical peak in prices, a high rental vacancy rate in inner areas but lower and falling vacancy rates in outer and regional locations with rents rising or falling in line with the underlying supply and demand equation being reflected in those vacancy rates.

We have never recommended property investment in inner Sydney and that position still has not changed. Equally it is unlikely that we would recommend regional locations with small populations for investment purposes. It is time though to start paying attention to outer suburbs and the greater Sydney satellite locations of which we prefer, for a variety of reasons, the Central Coast over the Blue Mountains, Campbelltown, or Wollongong.

The Central Coast and specifically Gosford has the shortest commute time into central Sydney and has been a star performer over the last 12 months with the rental vacancy rate falling from 5.1% in December 2019, just before the pandemic began, to a record low 0.8% today. The high vacancy rate in Gosford a year ago coincided with many new apartments coming into the market, which was of some concern at the time, but the pandemic and shifting market demand have cleaned up that problem rather swiftly.

Given the cyclical nature of supply and demand, the absolute optimum time to buy residential property only happens once every eight to twelve years. Despite this, in a long-term context, it is only the year just before and then 3 or so years after a cyclical peak that should be actively avoided. Greater Sydney is now approaching the end of that danger zone.

Clearly, careful property selection in the right locations will be essential over the next couple of years but we expect Australia's largest city to continue to provide sound long-term opportunity for investment.

In the short to medium term outer locations with perceived lifestyle benefits are likely to outperform inner areas.

Chapter 4

A SIMPLE PHILOSOPHY

WHY DO SOME INVESTORS FAIL?

Many people acknowledge that real estate, especially residential, is the best and safest investment of all. Why is it then that some appear to continually prosper from residential property investments and others fail to capitalise?

We have never failed to make a capital gain from residential property acquired for investment purposes in over sixty years of investment. There must be a system, or philosophy to follow that supports those who continually make money from property.

People have many stories to tell about their fluctuating fortunes in property. It is not unusual to hear of a homeowner who purchased their home and sold it within a few years and doubled their money. Others tell of bitter experience, where, compelled to sell, they have been unable to realise their original cost, or worse, were unable to sell for an amount sufficient to pay out their mortgage.

During economic recessions the media tend to feature stories of families in difficult circumstances. Some of the circumstances disclosed in these stories are tragic. Perhaps some of them are unavoidable. Some will get into difficulties no matter what the economy is doing.

The same applies to property investors. First time or inexperienced investors may find the need to sell, either because they have overcommitted or other economic circumstances caused a change of plans or financial difficulty.

If the market happens to be weak at the time, they may find the property hard to sell at a price that will recover their capital. They may also have to recover capital outlay over and above the original purchase price including losses incurred by negative gearing.

AVOIDING NEGATIVE GEARING PITFALLS

In other chapters of this book, negative gearing is discussed in more detail. The advantages are many, but there are down sides. How can these pitfalls be avoided or at least minimised?

At social gatherings, especially in Sydney, the subject of discussion among guests often turns to property. Typically, when property markets are strong someone will relate their story of good fortune in property only to be outdone by the next storyteller. Alternatively, during poor property markets each will outdo the other with stories of doom and gloom.

Probably because we are known as commentators and authors with a strong interest in property, the topic at gatherings we attend seems to turn to property more frequently than most other subjects.

On one such occasion, a guest told of buying a home in Sydney for a purchase price of $540,000. She told how she added a swimming pool as well as other improvements for a further cost of $80,000 increasing her total capital cost to $620,000. "I've had it on the market for the past twelve months" she related "and I can't even get an offer", "Don't talk to me about property" she continued "Property has to be the worst investment of all".

She could not be convinced otherwise, even though our experiences have been quite the opposite. Is it experience that counts? Inside information maybe? Being in the right place at the right time? Is it luck? All those elements can certainly help, but those who continue to make money in real estate seem to achieve success consistently. So, is there a formula or philosophy?

The answer is 'yes', and it is a simple one.

THE BUYING DECISION

When property values start to rise it generally follows an increase in rents. To those locked into the rental market, rising rents, at least for a period, become a way of life. This has a two-fold effect.

As rents rise the cost of servicing a loan falls below the cost of renting and prospective home buyers see the sense in acting before values rise further.

At the same time, investors are attracted to rental property purchase for the higher income yields caused by rising rents and relatively static values.

It is a powerful combination. Increased demand from both investors and home buyers at pretty much the same time. As the market grows in value more buyers are attracted, and the market moves into a stronger growth phase.

During a period of slow or static growth, the direct opposite occurs. Buyer demand slows, investors retreat and the market stalls.

It follows that the market moves from oversupply to under supply as demand ebbs and flows. When the market is moving up in value many feel compelled to enter the market, either to maximise their purchasing power before further growth, or to participate in the anticipated growth from escalating values.

In other chapters we show you how these values have moved over specific time periods in which buying property has been opportune and times when it is not.

When our friend who complained about the poor performance of her property was asked the timing of her purchase, we realised that she had purchased the home in 2004 and was trying to sell it throughout 2009.

By referring to the Sydney House Price chart you will see that 2004 was the peak of the property boom of the early noughties and 2009 was five years into the post-peak downturn with ongoing oversupply and static values.

She had bought at the top of the boom and was trying the sell in a slump. How could she possibly expect to achieve maximum results?

DON'T FOLLOW THE LEADER

This phenomenon is the "herd mentality" that is often talked about in investment circles. Large numbers of people buying when the market is rising and selling when it is falling. It is what most people do. If they did not, there would be no boom and no bust.

So, you can see how simple it is. By running counter to the herd instinct and doing the complete opposite, buying when the market is down and selling when it is up, the risk of loss is substantially reduced.

Referring back to the Sydney House Price chart, if our acquaintance had purchased in 1999 and sold in 2004 the result would have been completely different. Still a five-year holding period but five years earlier in the cycle. Based on the Sydney median house price her gain would have been 14.5% per annum compound instead of a loss of -1.6% per annum compound. A massive difference.

She purchased when she should have been selling and was selling when she should have been purchasing. That does not make a lot of sense. There is however, one more safeguard to be added. If you buy when the market is down and never sell, one more element of risk is eliminated.

A great deal of growth can be built into property at the time of purchase by correct timing, and of course, astute buying. If you never sell, you do not realise a loss during a subsequent downturn, and the property can be held for the next upturn which will eventually occur.

Always buy and never sell is a maxim we have lived by, and it does ensure the slow and successful accumulation of a substantial property estate.

Buying and selling residential property for personal occupation is a more selective situation than buying for investment. It is not always possible to time the sale of owner-occupied property to economic or property market circumstances. Transfers, loss of employment, health or marital problems push such control out of reach for many. The need to upgrade or downsize may influence timing. When we deal with our homes it is not a purely financial decision. But for investment property timing is more manageable.

Buying and selling in favourable markets is a reasonable objective. Even with owner occupied property one can make an argument for reasonable timing at both ends of the process however investment property demands good timing.

THE THREE MOST IMPORTANT ELEMENTS

Location, location, location has been repeatedly offered by some experts as the three most important factors in property selection. We think it is an oversimplification.

Whilst not denying the importance of location, it certainly is not the only important criteria. We would prefer to list the three most important elements as timing, financing, and location. And close on the heels of those are time (not the same as timing), information and patience. We discuss these qualities in other chapters.

For now, let's establish that the simplest and most important rule of real estate property purchase, is to buy when others sell, and sell when others buy. That is the area of opportunity. That is counter-cyclical property investment.

Chapter 5

THE ENORMOUS POTENTIAL OF LEVERAGE

RESIDENTIAL PROPERTY IS A WEALTH HAZARD

Before we consider the potential to build a secure property portfolio, we need to look at some of the mechanics of property investment.

If principles such as timing and financing and holding long term represent the philosophy, then leveraging capital growth represents the mechanics or engine room of property accumulation. This is what makes it work to the investors' advantage.

WHY PROPERTY OUTPERFORMS SHARES

The other mainstream form of investment that offers an alternative to property investment is the stock market. It has many of the qualities of property investment, and the same parameters can be applied to ensure profit and ensure security, but residential property does have some very definite advantages. Banks will lend more money, for longer periods, at lower interest rates, for residential property, then they will on any other commodity.

Before we explore that statement further, it should also be remembered that the returns from listed companies depends a great deal on the management by its executives and directors. It is a secondary market. The results are not in your hands.

With residential property a great deal more control can be exerted by the owner. Tenant selection criteria is in the owner's hands. Even if you use the services of a property manager, that can be easily changed if not satisfied. It is hard to change management of a corporation, especially for a small shareholder. Often even large shareholders have considerable trouble as we often see in some bitter proxy battles.

Being able to borrow more money on better terms for residential property investment, offers tremendous opportunities through leverage.

USING OTHER PEOPLE'S MONEY

Using other people's money, or borrowings, to improve our own profits is the basis of leverage. So how does it work?

A property is purchased for $100,000. The purchaser pays cash with no borrowings. The property increases in value by $10,000 to $110,000. The gain on capital invested would be 10%

Purchase Price	$100,000
Capital Gain	$10,000
Increased Value	$110,000
Gain on equity of $100,000	10%

Had the purchaser of the same property borrowed 50% of the purchase price the following result would have been achieved.

Purchase Price	$100,000
Borrowings	$50,000
Cash Outlay	$50,000
Capital Gain	$10,000
Increased Value	$110,000
Gain on equity of $50,000	20%

By borrowing 50% of the purchase price the purchaser reduced their cash outlay by half, but the gain of $10,000 remained the same. All the capital gain goes to the property owner. None to the lender.

What is most important is the gain on equity invested. The lender receives interest but none of the growth. As the purchaser/borrower you must pay interest, but the tenant, and the tax office are providing substantial assistance.

What if the purchaser borrowed more than 50% of the purchase price, say 80%?

Purchase Price	$100,000
Borrowings	$80,000
Cash Outlay	$20,000
Capital Gain	$10,000
Increased Value	$110,000
Gain on equity of $20,000	50%

HOW MULTI-MILLIONAIRES START FROM SMALL BEGINNINGS

The object of this book is to show you how to build a property estate for future security, be it to improve your lifestyle, or to retire in comfort. Many people who have embarked on such a program reach a point in assets build up that they no longer require to use any cash at all in subsequent purchases. They only need to use the equity created in previous acquisitions. When the value of a property where no cash at all has been outlaid increases, the capital gain cannot be calculated in percentage terms other than to say 1,000,000% to the nth degree on each such purchase.

This is how so many people have created property wealth, often from small beginnings. Once the process has commenced, it builds to the force of a train, and is relentless in building asset growth. If applied with some of the other ingredients we have outlined, the formula offers excellent rewards.

It is always proper to consider along with these principles the question of investor comfort and security. Borrowing to purchase property carries with it some risks.

When borrowing becomes negative, that is rental income and tax savings less expenses leave a shortfall, the borrower is exposed to a commitment that must be affordable. Not only can failure to meet such a commitment mean financial hardship but may result in the forced sale of the property in a poor market.

The question of negative income and gearing is discussed more fully in later chapters. It is sufficient here to outline the great potential that is exposed to the investor by using borrowings to increase capital gain through leverage.

Chapter 6

BECOME A PROPERTY MULTI-MILLIONAIRE IN 15 YEARS

ESCALATING GROWTH BY LEVERAGE

Do you want to substantially increase your net worth over the next ten to fifteen years? Let us assume you do, and seriously intend to pursue that objective. What is the process that you might undertake to achieve it?

You have decided that residential property is an appropriate means to achieve that end. As we have seen, one of the main principles in accumulating a substantial portfolio of property is by means of leverage. Leverage being the ability to own more property, and therefore receive more growth in property value by carefully planning to use other people's money, by borrowing on existing resources.

That implies using the right kind of borrowings wisely.

There are two kinds of other people's money. Let us make a real distinction by using the word debt for one kind, and the word borrowings for another. Debt describes money that we use to buy products or services that do not have lasting value or fall in value. When you use personal loans to buy cars, or use payment plans to buy furnishings, or you use a credit card to go on a holiday, that is debt.

You are just spending money you have not earned yet. You are not acquiring something that has lasting value or increases in value.

Straight after the holiday, it has no value at all, other than memories. Whilst holidays are important, even when you cannot leave your home state as was the case through much of 2020, they do not secure our financial future.

We use the word borrowings when we use other people's money to buy something that does have lasting value or will increase in value. That is a very real distinction. Debt is a negative word. Not too many people wake up in the morning thinking "I'm going to get some debt today". Borrowings sounds much more positive.

The distinction is clear. There are good and not-so-good reasons to borrow money.

With that in mind, how do you apply these principles to add substantially to your net worth over the next fifteen years without putting yourself at undue risk, or doing things that cause you to lie awake at night?

HOW ONE COUPLE CREATED A MULTI-MILLION DOLLAR ESTATE

A CASE STUDY

This case study appears exactly as it did in the original version of this book almost twenty-five years ago.

James and Susan purchased their first home in Sydney in June 1987. The home they purchased was a modest cottage, worth close to the median value for houses in Sydney at the time. In this case study, James and Susan are a fictitious couple we will use to show how, by safe and conservative planning, modest beginnings can be escalated into substantial wealth and security.

They paid $83,000 to purchase their first home, with a cash deposit of $21,000, part of which was used to pay stamp duty and legal costs, and a home loan from their bank of $66,000.

ORIGINAL HOME PURCHASE (TEN YEARS AGO)	
Purchase Price	$83,000
Purchase Costs	$4,000
Total Cost	$87,000
Cash Deposit	$21,000
Mortgage	$66,000
Total Funds	$87,000

After living in that home for more than ten years, and in line with the actual growth in Sydney values over that period, their home has now increased in value to $220,000. They have reduced their home loan from $66,000 to $50,000. As it is a principal and interest loan, it has not reduced quickly. The payments on the loan in those early years have mainly been interest. Today they have equity, which is the value of the property less the amount they owe the bank, or anyone else, of $170,000.

HOME POSITION TODAY	
Value	$220,000
Less Mortgage	$50,000
Present Equity	$170,000

The actual result they have achieved in financial terms, is that equity has grown from $21,000 when they purchased the property ten years ago, to $170,000 today. An excellent result, but of course, all they own is the same home at its increased value.

GROWTH IN HOME EQUITY	
Original equity	$21,000
Asset growth (and loan reduction)	$149,000
Present Equity	$170,000

The Next Ten Years

If we project their position today ten years into the future and increase the value of their home at say 8% per annum, it will increase to $475,000. It will then be just over twenty years since they originally purchased their home, and they would have paid off the home loan. They would have equity in their home of $475,000, most of which, other than the loan of $66,000 which they paid off over the period, was achieved by natural market growth. No major renovations or rezoning or change of land use. Just the increase in value over time. In this example we have used an 8% growth rate.

HOME EQUITY IN TEN YEARS FROM NOW	
Value of home today	$220,000
Projected growth @ 8% per annum compound	$225,000
Projected value in ten years	$475,000
Mortgage in ten years	NIL
Projected equity in ten years	$475,000

In ten years, with a property value of $475,000, they could sell and buy a cheaper home and bank the difference, but as their home is in the median price range, that would mean settling for significantly inferior accommodation. They may even have to rent to have a reasonable nest egg if they were to retire at that time.

Adding to Growth Potential

Alternatively, they could do something now to add to their growth potential over the next ten years by using their property as collateral and borrowing to acquire additional property, which could be rented as an investment, with tax benefits, and most importantly, would also grow in value.

James and Susan decide on the latter plan and approach their bank manager for a loan to purchase investment property. But what are the risks? The first rule of investment is to protect existing capital. The bank would look at James and Susan's position and should be happy to lend them up to 90% of their homes value of $220,000. At this level of borrowings, they would have to pay for mortgage insurance which protects the bank's position. But they want to remain conservative, especially as a first-time investment, and decide to borrow only 75% of their homes present value. Banks do not usually require mortgage insurance at this level of borrowing, as they perceive minimal risk, especially on investment in residential property.

Avoiding Blue Sky

If protecting our capital is our number one rule, then avoiding either "blue sky" optimism, or taking too "gung-ho" an approach to investment are important points to keep in mind.

The bank agreed to lend them 75% of the value of their home today, a $165,000 loan. But they still have a balance of $50,000, owing on their existing mortgage. If that $50,000 is deducted it leaves a borrowable amount of $115,000 which could be used as a deposit for a further investment property. The bank then must establish that they can afford to service the total loan out of their income including the rent from the new investment property and the potential tax savings which would result from investment ownership. Providing those tests are met, the bank would lend them $115,000 "for any worthwhile purpose", to use a bank expression, in this case, as the deposit for another property purchase.

If James and Susan also borrow 75% of the value of the new investment property they intend to acquire, that would give them a total borrowing power of $385,000, which could be used to purchase properties worth $365,000 after allowing for acquisition costs such as stamp duty and legal fees. The next week they could go shopping for a property or properties up to $365,000 in total value.

BORROWING FOR INVESTMENT PURPOSES	
Current value of home	$220,000
Increase borrowings to 75% of present value	$165,000
Less, current borrowings	($50,000)
Further borrowings obtainable on existing home	$115,000
Plus, loan on new properties at 75% of purchase price	$270,000
Total borrowing power	$385,000
Funds available for further purchases after purchase costs	$365,000

You can see in the following figures with their new mortgage of $385,000 for investment property, with a value of $365,000 after allowing for stamp duty, legal fees and borrowing costs, which equate to around 5% of the purchase price of a median priced property, plus their home and existing mortgage, their total property holdings have increased to $585,000 with borrowings of $435,000.

POSITION WITH NEW PROPERTIES			
	HOME	INVESTMENT PROPERTIES	TOTAL
Value	$220,000	$365,000	$585,000
Borrowings	$50,000	$385,000	$435,000
Equity	$170,000	($20,000)	$150,000

What they have done is increase their assets and liabilities, giving them greater exposure to future increases in values. Now they will receive capital growth on property worth $585,000.

The First Five Years

If they then do nothing for the next five years, what would their situation be? Applying the same principles and assuming values have increased at an average 8% per annum, their home would have increased to $323,000. We can assume that they have continued repayments on their home loan as they have done in the past, increasing their equity, and reducing the mortgage.

POSITION IN FIVE YEARS FROM NOW			
	HOME	INVESTMENT PROPERTIES	TOTAL
Value	$323,000	$536,000	$859,000
Borrowings	$24,000	$385,000	$409,000
Equity	$299,000	$151,000	$450,000

The investment properties have increased at 8% per annum to $536,000. They still have the loan they took out to buy the properties at $385,000. If it were a principal and interest loan it would have reduced a little increasing the equity. We will assume that they borrowed interest only for investment purposes, so their total property holdings have increased to $859,000 with loans of $409,000 which is under 50% of the value of their properties. Looking at the total picture, this is a conservative level of borrowings. Their equity has increased to $450,000.

They have virtually achieved in five years what would have taken ten if they had just continued paying off their home and left their equity passively non-productive. By putting that equity to work within conservative limits, they have substantially improved their net worth. This could be achieved at relatively low ongoing cost, which is covered in detail in the next chapter. The actual ongoing cost to James and Susan works out to be less than leasing the average family car worth say $28,000 and which will fall in value, compared to owning $365,000 in additional property which will rise in value. There is no comparison - it is chalk and cheese.

After that first five-year period, James and Susan are very satisfied with the results of their first property investment. They go back to the bank to show their manager what they have achieved and seek to borrow for further investment.

After the First Five Years

They have property worth $859,000. If they again increase or "top-up" their borrowings to 75% of that higher value, they could borrow an additional $235,000. If that $235,000 again becomes the released equity from current properties to act as deposit to buy more property on which they borrow 75% of value, they would have a purchasing power, after acquisition costs, of $785,000.

THE NEXT FIVE YEARS BORROWING FOR FURTHER INVESTMENT	
Current value of property	$859,000
Increase borrowings to 75% of present value	$644,000
Less, current borrowings	($409,000)
Further borrowings obtainable on existing home	$235,000
Plus, loan on new properties at 75% of purchase price	$550,000
Funds available for further purchases after purchase costs	$785,000

James and Susan now buy another three properties at around $250,000 each, or any combination up to $745,000 after allowing for costs. Remember property values have increased generally by that time. That brings their new overall position to property holdings of $1,604,000 with borrowings of $1,194,000 and equity of $410,000.

YEAR FIVE - WITH NEW PROPERTIES ACQUIRED			
	HOME	INVESTMENT PROPERTIES	TOTAL
Value	$323,000	$1,280,000	$1,640,000
Borrowings	$24,000	$1,170,000	$1,194,000
Equity	$299,000	$300,000	$410,000

After Ten Years of Escalating

If they do nothing for another five years and then reassess the situation, their home has increased to $475,000 as we first calculated it would over the ten-year period. They have now paid out the balance of their home loan, which five years ago was down to $24,000. The investment properties have increased to $1.88 million; the loans are unchanged at $1.17 million. The total value of the properties they are holding is $2.355 million, with borrowings of $1.194 million. Their equity has increased to $1.161 million.

POSITION AFTER TEN YEARS			
	HOME	INVESTMENT PROPERTIES	TOTAL
Value	$475,000	$1,880,000	$2,355,000
Borrowings	NIL	$1,194,000	$1,194,000
Equity	$475,000	$686,000	$1,161,000

If they had kept their home, made no investment at all, and paid off their mortgage, the equity would have been only $475,000 not $1,161,000, as the case study demonstrates. They have increased their net worth by $1 million within ten years.

They then review the situation again. With a total property value of $2.35 million, they bring borrowings back up to 75% or $1.76 million, less the current loans of $1.194 million. They can then borrow another $572,000, as long as it can be serviced by a combination of rents, tax benefits and personal income. It becomes another feasible step without high risk. That would give them a total purchasing power of $1.906 million. This time James and Susan can acquire a whole building of new apartments for that sum. With those purchases and another five years, a total of fifteen years from now, growth on James and Susan's property portfolio has been substantial.

A Multi-Millionaire After Fifteen Years

A MULTI-MILLIONAIRE AFTER FIFTEEN YEARS			
	HOME	INVESTMENT PROPERTIES	TOTAL
Value	$698,000	$5,563,000	$6,260,000
Borrowings	NIL	$3,100,000	$3,100,000
Equity	$698,000	$2,463,000	$3,161,000

By keeping borrowings to a level that any professional investor, or any financial adviser would regard as reasonably conservative, that is topping up to no more than 75%, they have managed to enhance their lifestyle, wealth, and security, far beyond that achievable from income and savings.

Slowing the Pace to Retirement

James and Susan could continue to add to their portfolio and probably will. Now retirement is in sight and even though they are now only in their mid-fifties, they are starting to think about retirement income. They will probably continue to buy more property, possibly even encourage and assist their children to invest in property, but at a slower pace than before.

This will allow overall borrowings to progressively fall as a proportion of value and allow the portfolio to start generating net income in their hands as rents exceed interest and expenses. If they wanted to speed up that process, they could sell a few properties and use the net sale proceeds to reduce borrowings on the remaining properties. This would allow even more net income to flow to them.

Not everybody wants borrowings of more than $3,000,000, or even need a net worth of almost $3,200,000, but many people have achieved those results. This is one of the most common ways that people build wealth. Creating or earning a large income does not necessarily build wealth, accumulating assets does.

THE KEY PRINCIPLES

In this study, James and Susan have been relatively conservative. They have patiently created a large portfolio of property over time. The properties were prudently financed for investment purposes, and throughout this example we have assumed less growth in property values than has been the case in the past although with inflation falling that may not be the case for the foreseeable future. We will explain in a later chapter why the relationship between inflation and the rate of growth is what really matters.

Our example has seen them review and invest every five years, for ease of example. In practice they may have reviewed their situation more frequently and acquired property sooner than this case study provides, which would in turn enhance the result they were able to achieve.

We have used a constant growth rate. As this book reveals, market cycles do not always provide a constant level of growth. At times values will increase at higher or lower rates, so increasing the investors opportunities to buy at the best time in the cycle to enhance growth. James and Susan will also vary their purchasing programme depending on changes to their income, prevailing interest rates and rent levels, hastening, or slowing their purchases as circumstances permit.

There are people who would do more than James and Susan, adopting a more aggressive, higher risk approach. Keeping what we do with our investments to a level that we are comfortable with, so that we can sleep at night, is just as important as any other consideration. We could do more, or certainly do less, according to our individual objectives, resources, lifestyle, and comfort zone.

GETTING STARTED FROM NOTHING

The prospects for James and Susan achieving property wealth in this case study depends on them having purchased their first home ten years previously with a present build-up of equity to launch them into an asset building program.

MONEY MANAGEMENT

Not everyone is in that fortunate position. With family responsibilities or a newly acquired mortgage and twenty years of mortgage payments ahead, the task to acquire a first investment property may seem a formidable one.

For most, the first property purchase will be the family home, and for the majority, that will be the right course to follow, but not necessarily so.

We point out that it is possible to borrow more money to purchase rental investment property than to buy an owner-occupied home. The rental income and tax benefits from investment property increases affordability in the eyes of the lender. This makes for better access into the market. Often for singles or double income couples, an investment property may be the best first purchase.

A FOOT IN THE MARKET

Saving a deposit for a first home remains the first and foremost priority for most people starting out. You need to get a foot in the market, or it will pass you by. Sometimes the struggle can be difficult but struggle you must. That can mean sacrifices, hard work, or going without. It is a simple choice.

Once you are on the first rung, acquiring your second property will be the next goal. Sure, it may also seem tough, but the rewards are worth the struggle.

If moving from home ownership to property investor proves onerous, you still have the same option that James and Susan had. It took them ten years to make their first investment. Instead of achieving property wealth in fifteen years, it may take twenty-five years.

Youth should be on your side. James and Susan took ten years before starting to use the accumulated equity in their home to set them on a path to financial security. Maybe they could have started sooner.

This raises a common question. How do we know when to invest? Do we pay off the home loan entirely, wait until it is significantly reduced, or is there a magic formula? Whilst there is not a hard and fast rule, you might consider this.

There is no doubt home loans should be reduced as quickly as reasonably possible. The payments are not tax deductible and therefore the cost is high, but only to a point.

If you adopt the view that the interest on your home loan represents the cost to you of providing a roof over your head, then there is a way to work out at what point you might start to invest in additional property.

If the interest is equal to, or less than, the rental value of your home, then you have reduced your home loan to less than its "shelter" value and you could consider investment.

If the interest is above the amount you would have to pay to rent your home, then continuing to use disposable income to reduce your loan until it does reach that point is probably the best course of action.

It is not hard to establish the rental value of your home. You could have a local real estate agent assess it for you - it is a normal part of the service they offer. Alternatively, it is easy to search online rental advertisements in your area to establish an approximate rental value.

The interest on your loan should include just that, interest only, not the total payments you make which would normally include a repayment of principal component.

When James and Susan first set out on the property investment path, they applied this test:

Home current market value	$220,000
Home Loan Balance	$50,000
Interest at say 5%	$2,500
Rental value at $250 per week	$13,000 per annum

Their interest component was well under the rental value of their house and indicated they could probably have comfortably invested for the first time much sooner than they did.

By waiting, the built-up equity in their home remains passive for longer when it could be leveraging them into ownership of additional property on which they will receive capital growth. The benefit of more growth would far outweigh the non-deductibility of interest on their already less than "shelter" value home loan.

There are other principles you will read in this book, that may speed the property accumulation process. Buying at the right time, in the right place, with the right funding, and the right tax advantages, could reduce the time factor substantially.

Chapter 7

THE TAX ADVANTAGES OF RESIDENTIAL PROPERTY

BUILDING DEPRECIATION ALLOWANCES

Any residential dwelling which commenced construction in Australia after 17 July 1985, qualifies for an annual building allowance of 2.5% of the original construction cost.

Let us take an example property which is relatively new. Of its $220,000 purchase price, around 50% will be the actual cost of construction, the balance will be the land value. Of the $110,000 building cost, 2.5% of that figure can be taken as an annual tax deduction, that is $2,750, every year for forty years.

Purchase Price	$220,000
Construction Cost	$110,000
2.5% Allowance	$2,750 per annum

What we are doing is writing off the entire cost of the building over time. As we said, any residential property that is owned by an investor for rental purposes, and was built after July 1985, qualifies for that allowance. This factor makes newer properties significantly more attractive than properties that do not qualify for the depreciation allowance.

TAX DEFERRED INCOME FROM RESIDENTIAL PROPERTY

We should clearly understand this. One of the investment properties James and Susan purchased had an income or rental of $250 per week or $13,000 per year. Of that $13,000, the 2.5% building depreciation allowance of $2,750 causes 21.15% of gross rental income to be sheltered from tax in that year. It is effectively a tax deferral as the building allowance deduction reduces the cost base for future capital gains tax calculation when and if you do sell at some point in the future.

Rent @ $250 per week	$13,000 per annum
Building Depreciation Allowance 2.5% of $110,000	$2,750 per annum
% of Gross Income Tax Free	21.15%

Back in 1985, two things happened, the building allowance was introduced, but so was capital gains tax. Capital gains tax takes away, the building allowance gives back.

If you buy a property today for investment purposes that was built before July 1985, you pay capital gains tax if you sell it, but you do not get the trade-off benefit of the building allowance. As it is based on the original construction cost of the building, even a ten-year-old property would have a significantly lower construction cost than a new building. There is a real distinction between older and newer property for investment purposes. At least from a cashflow perspective, newer is clearly better.

On just one modestly priced property that is $110,000 less taxable income Susan and James will pay tax on over the life of the building, calculated at $2,750 per annum by forty years. At the highest marginal tax rate, this would be a total tax saving over the life of the building of around $50,000.

TAX SAVINGS FROM ADDITIONAL DEPRECIATION

Another major allowance or tax concession is depreciation on the fixtures and fittings in the dwelling, items such as the carpets, blinds, light fittings, the hot water system etc. In this case study they amount to a further deduction of $1,700. The method of calculating the amount of this deduction is fully covered in the chapter "How to Establish Net Yield".

BORROWING EXPENSES

James and Susan then have the borrowing costs, that is the fees they paid the bank when they borrowed the money, loan application fees, stamp duty on mortgages, and mortgage insurance (if applicable). There are other statutory charges, lawyers search fees and sundry out of pocket expenses. On James and Susan's purchase that amounted to a total of $3,300. That sum can be deducted for tax purposes over the term of the loan, or five years whichever is less. So, if it is a three-year fixed loan, which you renew, or re-finance at the end of the term, then you can deduct one third of all of those bank charges, in each of those three years, giving a deduction of $1,100 in the first twelve-month period.

INTEREST TAX DEDUCTIONS

James and Susan borrowed against existing assets when they purchased their first investment property. Initially it was their own home. Even though they borrowed on their home which is not an income earning property, the interest expense is deductible for income tax purposes as it is capital used to purchase other income producing property. It can be deducted against total income from investment property or salary.

Any expense that occurs in earning or generating income is deductible against total income for tax purposes and interest on borrowing makes up a major portion of those expenses.

As James and Susan continued to escalate their real estate holdings they continued to borrow against their growing assets. The cost of which is deductible against income.

For the purposes of this case study James and Susan borrowed 75% of existing assets which includes all properties acquired to that date, which represents 100% of the purchase cost of the newly acquired property, even though some of the borrowed amount is secured against their own home or other property.

THE FIRST TIME INVESTOR

It might be appropriate at this time to look at the first-time investor and place him or her in James and Susan's shoes. James and Susan purchased a home ten years ago for $83,000 plus costs. Today that home has increased in value to $220,000. They have a mortgage of $50,000 leaving equity of $170,000.

HOME POSITION TODAY

Value	$220,000
Less Mortgage	$50,000
Present Equity	$170,000

They used that equity to borrow further funds for reinvestment. They established that they could without undue risk borrow 75% of the property's value or $165,000. They still had a mortgage of $50,000 providing $115,000 of new borrowings towards the down payment on further investments.

With $115,000 as a down payment they could borrow a further 75% of the value of any new acquisitions which works out to be $270,000, giving them a total of $385,000 less acquisition costs to spend on further purchases.

BORROW FOR FURTHER PROPERTY INVESTMENT

Current Value of Home	$220,000
Increase borrowings to 75% of value	$165,000
Less, current home loan	($50,000)
Further borrowings obtainable on new acquisitions	$115,000
Plus, loan on new properties at 75% of purchase price	$270,000
Funds available for further purchase	$385,000
Less, Acquisition Costs	$20,000
	$365,000

The interest charges on the total borrowings of $385,000 would be a deduction against their total income, that is from all investments and salaries. At say 5% interest that would be a tax deduction for taxable income assessment of $19,250 per annum.

EXPERT ADVICE

Taxation issues in relation to property and property investment can be complicated and often require interpretation based on individual circumstances. We recommend you consult your accountant or tax agent for specific tax advice.

NEGATIVE GEARING NEEDS GROWTH

Whilst negative gearing has been the catch cry of property markets over the last fifty years it is not a subject we have dwelt on in this book.

It was not until Fred Johnson's book "How to Get Real Estate Rich" published in 1969 that the general property investment community came to understand how it could be effectively used in reducing assessable income.

When the expenses from property exceed the income after all deductions including interest, the negative result can be offset against other income earned by the property investor to reduce total tax. Even though that income is not from property. It may be from salary, fixed interest investment, shares or other taxable sources.

This tax saving, when coupled with leveraged growth, can have exceptional results. If you refer to the chapter on leverage, you will see how using borrowed funds multiplies the growth factor.

The reason we do not make more of this is because negative gearing as such produces a loss. Even though the after-tax result is minimised it is still a loss and is only recaptured if the value of the investment grows over time.

Even minimal growth when leveraged can make a negatively geared property provide excellent results as we have seen in the case study of James and Susan, where they turned the equity in their home into millions over fifteen years.

But you must have growth. No amount of negative gearing will overcome the fact that you are subsidising the investment if the property does not grow in value. That said, the additional tax benefits of residential real estate investment can minimise the risks of negative gearing and make it stand out against other forms of investment.

If one of James and Susan's property purchases was at a price of $250,000, allowing for acquisition costs they would have a loan of say $260,000. Assuming they borrowed all the funds required to complete the purchase, the annual deductible interest expense would be $13,000 at a rate of say 5%.

When combined with the other deductions available on residential property it creates a significant total deduction against rental and other income.

CASH DEDUCTIONS	YEAR ONE
Loan Interest	$13,000
Property expenses including vacancy	$3,700
Total Cash Expenses	$16,700
NON CASH DEDUCTIONS	
Building Depreciation allowance	$3,250
Borrowing expenses first 3 years	$800
Depreciation on fixtures and fittings	$2,300
Total Non-Cash Expenses	$6,360
TOTAL DEDUCTIONS	$23,050

That gives them total tax deductions including interest, property expenses, building allowance, depreciation on fixtures and fittings, and borrowing costs of $23,050 in the first year of ownership.

You will notice in the table we have divided the deductions into cash and non-cash items. The cash items are things you physically must pay for like loan interest to the bank and property outgoings to councils, insurers, property management fees etc.

The non-cash items are deductions or allowances that you can take up in your tax return but do not outlay cash to receive such as the building allowance. It also includes the amortisation of the borrowing expenses paid at point of purchase and depreciation on the fixtures and fittings within the property. Keep in mind depreciation is helpful from a cashflow perspective but at some point, those depreciable items will need to be physically replaced.

CASH COST		
Gross rental income		$13,000
Less, total cash deductions		$16,900
Net cash cost		($3,900)
Less, non-cash deductions		
Building depreciation allowance	$3,250	
Depreciation on fixtures and fittings	$2,300	
Borrowing expenses	$800	$6,350
Net loss for tax purposes		($10,050)

If we bring the total picture together, they will have rental income of $13,000, a cash shortfall before tax of $3,900 and a tax loss on paper of $10,050.

It is the $10,050 net loss on paper that reduces their taxable income. If they earn $70,000 in taxable income, that income would be reduced for tax assessment by $10,050 reducing the tax they would otherwise pay. At the applicable marginal tax rate, they would receive a tax credit or a tax saving of $3,367 in that year.

	BEFORE PROPERTY INVESTMENT	WITH PROPERTY INVESTMENT
Gross Income	$70,000	$70,000
Net loss from property	NIL	$10,050
Taxable Income	$70,000	$59,950
Tax	$14,297	$10,930
Tax Saving	$0	$3,367

THE TOTAL TAX SAVINGS

Keep in mind that they have outlaid cash of $3,900, but have saved tax of $3,367, so the net cost of holding that property over the first year is $533.

Cash Outlay	$3,900
Tax Saving	$3,367
Net cost to hold	$533

The after-tax cost of $533 represents less than 1% of their income of $70,000 per annum. That represents a form of forced savings by accepting the commitment and obliging them to meet the shortfall. The property is expected to increase in value by substantially more than that amount, so it is a suitable form of forced saving.

In this example the after-tax cost is low and manageable but that is not always the case. In periods of higher interest rates or lower rental yields the after-tax cost can be significantly higher. In those circumstances, carrying the cash outlay through the year can be a burden even though you expect a large tax refund. You can elect not to carry that outlay.

HOW TO FUND THE CASH SHORTFALL

There is provision in the tax act, whereby, as soon as you purchase the property, you can arrange to reduce the tax being deducted from your salary if you are a PAYG taxpayer. This involves completing an online form with details of your salary income, the rent that you expect to receive, estimated expenses including the non-cash deductions, and the net loss on the investment.

Generally, within 28 days you should receive a letter from the tax office, authorising the amount of tax currently being deducted from your PAYE income, to be reduced by the amount of estimated tax saving which in this example is $3,367 for the year.

With that in place you are only outlay the net amount over the course of the year. It is a simple process and avoids the fifteen months or so delay in recovering the tax benefits or refund from the Tax Office.

It is necessary to lodge annually, but it is simple to do online yourself or your tax agent can do it for you.

Some people prefer to carry the cost because they like to receive a large refund cheque at the end of the year. There is nothing wrong with that, just keep in mind that what they are really doing is lending money to the Federal Government interest free.

THE BANK

The income that James and Susan needed to borrow the funds for this property was about $52,000 per year. Their annual gross income of around $70,000 allowed them to comfortably borrow the full amount $260,000. As the loan was exclusively for investment purposes the bank, in assessing the application, considered the rental income from the property and the tangible savings from the tax deductibility of interest on the loan and other property expenses.

You can usually borrow substantially more for investment purposes, than you can for home ownership.

KEEPING INVESTMENT WITHIN THE COMFORT ZONE

It makes sense to use available cash, income, and savings as efficiently as possible to maximise investment results but within conservative constraints. Tax instalments can be adjusted to assist cash flow if needed, but even more importantly, whatever you do, ensure that it is at a comfortable level of commitment.

At the outset you must know how much you can borrow. There are a couple of things to note. Firstly, you can borrow more for investment purposes, than you can for home ownership. Second, there will be a large variation between banks in how much they will lend you.

The reason we believe it is so important to know much you can borrow is to avoid borrowing too much. We are fans of the idea that you should never actually borrow more than 75% of your maximum borrowing capacity at any point in time. Keep it moving forward but keep it comfortable.

INTEREST ONLY VERSES PRINCIPAL & INTEREST BORROWINGS

Whether to borrow money for a property investment purchase on an "interest only", or "principal and interest" basis is one of the most common questions we have been asked over the years and had to be addressed by James and Susan when they decided to invest. The answer is a crystal clear "it depends". Firstly, let us define our terms.

Interest Only

Offered by all major lenders, the interest only loan is the form of borrowing most often used by property investors.

It is a form of borrowing which is usually on fixed terms of between one and five years, at an interest rate fixed for the elected term, and on which only interest payments are made during the term of the loan.

There is no reduction of principal or "paying off" the loan along the way.

At the end of the term the principal is either re-financed for a further fixed term, or reverts to a principal and interest basis, or is repaid. A part repayment with the balance re-financed is another option.

If a fixed rate fixed term loan is wholly or partly repaid before expiration of the term, there may be early repayment penalties where the prevailing market rates are lower than your fixed rate. Generally, the longer the remaining term of the loan you are repaying, the higher the "break cost" penalties.

This is one reason why we tend to prefer three-year fixed loans as a middle ground option just in case a sale and or repayment of the loan needs to occur for any reason.

Only the interest component of any payments you make on an investment loan are tax deductible. Therefore, on an interest only loan, the whole of the amount you pay each month is tax deductible.

This has obvious financial and cash flow benefits simply by causing the property to require less of your income to hold it, and possibly more importantly, the fixed rate removes, at least for the fixed period, any surprises or discomfort that movements in interest rates can cause.

Principal & Interest

The classic use of Principal and Interest borrowings is the typical home loan.

When we borrow to buy a home, to some extent what we are doing is, rather than renting a home, we rent the money with which to buy one. And just like the cost of renting a house, the rent (interest) we pay on the money is not tax deductible and therefore expensive.

We generally embrace the notion that home loans should be reduced or as quickly as possible, although as we saw earlier, we do not necessarily need to totally pay off our home loan before we start to invest.

When principal and interest loans are used for property investment purposes different rules apply. The interest component is tax deductible, however, the proportion we pay to reduce or repay the principal is not.

With a typical twenty-five or thirty-year term, the principal is progressively repaid over the term of the loan. In the early years most of the regular payments are in fact interest. In the later years, the amount of principal repayment we are making increases as the amount of interest we are paying falls in line with the reducing principal.

Principal and interest loans are usually offered with a variable interest rate. That is, the rate can rise and fall in line with financial markets which can be influenced by a myriad of factors from monetary policy to exchange rates, to market competition.

MISCONCEPTIONS ABOUT INVESTMENT LOANS

There are many misconceptions about both types of loans as they relate to property investment. Some common ones include:

"Reducing the principal increases equity"

Some people see an advantage in reducing the principal as a way of increasing equity in the property. You could view it as a form of forced saving, but technically it does not actually create new equity as the funds used are yours in the first place. Only an increase in the market value of the property can do that.

"How do we ever own it?"

If we borrow interest only for investment purposes it is because we are maximising use of our available income, to own as much property as we reasonably can, to receive the future benefit of capital growth. A shift in thinking away from the mind set of "paying-off" a home loan is required.

"What happens at the end of an interest only loan?"

These days when we borrow on a fixed rate fixed term basis the loan is usually written as a longer twenty-five or thirty-year term but fixed for an initial period. Whilst it is usually straight-forward to re-fix for a further period, if nothing is done at the end of the fixed period it usually automatically reverts to a variable rate principal and interest basis.

DECISION

In deciding whether to borrow interest only or principal and interest, it comes down to a balance between financial discipline and temperament.

If you are reasonably organised, efficient, and ambitious then there is absolutely no doubt interest only loans were designed with you in mind.

If at the other end of the spectrum you are a worrier, less ambitious or disorganised, then a principal and interest loan could be the way for you.

A slight exception to the rule could be if your home loan is totally paid off and you do not plan to redraw funds in the future, then borrowing for investment on a principal and interest basis probably does no major harm.

Borrowing on a principal and interest basis for investment while still paying off a home loan is usually inappropriate.

CONCLUSION

As we said - it depends. Interest only is financially more efficient, however if you cannot see past the idea that only principal and interest is within your comfort zone, then you are probably still better off doing that than not investing at all.

Chapter 8

DEPRECIATION - THE BIG SLEEPER

BUILDINGS LOSE VALUE

In 1969 we published a book called "How to Get Real Estate Rich". One chapter dealt with depreciation or should we say the lack of it. The United States has for many years allowed property investors to depreciate real estate improvements, that is, to allow the cost of buildings to be depreciated annually as an expense against income. The Americans went even further by allowing that depreciation to be accelerated down to, in certain circumstances, a four-year period.

The plain fact is that buildings do lose value with age. The cost of replacement will in most cases exceed the value of older property. That stands to reason. Why should it not be a charge against income?

The land on which the building sits invariably increases in value. It is the land that increases in value, as buildings decline in value to less than replacement cost and ultimately to zero.

At the time we published "How to Get Real Estate Rich" we took the matter of depreciation on property to the then Minister of Finance in the sitting coalition conservative party. We received a good hearing and acknowledgment that the idea of allowing depreciation deductions for tax purposes on property had not been considered previously, that it had merit and would be put to the government of the day.

At the same time many on the opposition benches and their supporters were lobbying for a capital gains tax. The supporters of a capital gains tax had failed to appreciate the justifiable and fair argument that it was not reasonable to tax gain if at the same time depreciation on improvements was not recognised as a tax allowance.

If not, it meant that capital gains tax would be applied to improvements that were really experiencing a capital loss. Ultimately it was the Hawke Labor Government with Paul Keating as Treasurer that in September 1985 introduced a capital gains tax.

Although capital gains tax applies to gains on any commodity, with some exceptions for personal property and now small businesses, we will confine our attention here to property.

When capital gains tax became tax law in 1985 several concessions came with it. The family home or principal place of residence was exempt from assessment under the legislation. Although expected, it was a major advantage for property owners.

The Government recognised the inequity of the tax unless it was accompanied by a depreciation allowance and introduced an allowable figure of 4% of the cost of improvements. In a further display of fairness, the capital gains tax and depreciation allowance would only apply to property purchased, after the day of announcement. But there was a poison pill. Until that date all interest on borrowed funds used to make the purchase were fully and totally deductible against income.

GOVERNMENT INTERFERENCE IN MARKET FORCES

The new provisions were to quarantine interest and other deductions to a break-even figure. Interest charges when added to other outgoings such as rates, insurance, body corporate fees, management charges etc. were only allowed to be deducted as an expense up to the figure that represented a break even return. This effectively eliminated negative gearing which was the intention.

Until then losses over and above break even could be offset against other assessable income providing a favourable tax advantage. The idea was to shut down the use of negative gearing as it was viewed as an unfair advantage to higher income earners. It backfired. Those who had entered the residential property market and taken advantage of negative gearing lost enthusiasm and those who had not already entered the market had much less inducement to do so.

Who was going to provide the residential accommodation for the 30% of the population who choose or need to rent? A shortage of rental property developed. Residential rents went through the roof. Many investors sold out of the residential market. Long queues of tenants formed outside real estate agents' offices and on the spot rental auctions were held with the lease being granted to the highest rental bidder.

The legislation was hurting those it had sought to help, increasing rents to levels that were out of reach for average families. The rate of new construction slowed exacerbating the situation. Government could also see that more public housing would be required at high cost to taxpayers.

In September 1987, the Government amended the law. The quarantining of losses was repealed and as an offset the building depreciation rate of 4% per annum on the cost of improvements was reduced to 2.5% per annum.

To return interest and expenses to fully deductible status was a relief to the market and giving up the difference between 4% per annum depreciation and 2.5% per annum was not a big price to pay.

WHY IS BUILDING DEPRECIATION SUCH A VALUABLE BENEFIT?

2.5% per annum does not sound like a large amount but 2.5% of the cost of construction of property can amount to up to a third or more of the income of the property being effectively tax deferred until the property is sold.

We expand on the use and benefits of building depreciation in other chapters. For now, we should look at the basic principle and substantial benefit.

A purchaser buys a home unit at a cost of $200,000 and the cost of construction is established at $100,000. It is newly constructed and qualifies for 2.5% per annum building depreciation. The rental value is determined at $200 per week.

Cost of purchase		$200,000
Cost of improvements excluding furnishings and fittings		$100,000
Income $250 per week		$13,000 per annum
Outgoings:		
Rates	$950	
Body Corporate Levies	$1,000	
Insurance	$220	
Property Management	$1,200	
Vacancy Allowance	$260	
Repairs Replacements	$270	
Total Outgoings:		$3,900
Net income before depreciation		$9,100

The depreciable construction cost or was established at $100,000 so the annual depreciation allowance is 2.5% of that sum or $2,500 per annum.

The $2,500 is a non-cash outgoing. It does not come out of your pocket nor is it an actual cost out of income, it is purely a tax concession which shelters valuable cash flow.

Income	$13,000
Outgoings	$3,900
Net income before depreciation	$9,100
Less depreciation	$100,000 (original construction cost)
Building allowance	$2,500
Taxable Income	$6,600

The depreciation allowance of $2,500 per annum in this example causes 24% of the gross rental income to be tax deferred. The allowance continues each year for the first forty years of the property's life. A total tax deduction of $100,000.

A related tax benefit is depreciation allowances on fittings, fixtures and furniture including the cost of carpets, blinds, light fitting, curtains, hot water systems, ovens, ranges and many more. Detailed tables of depreciation schedules are available online. Essentially all these items have a defined economic life over which you may deduct a proportion of their value each year.

Chapter 9

ESTABLISHING A NET RETURN

The net return or yield represents the net income profit on the property as a percentage of the capital employed. In other words, the net yield on capital employed, or the earning rate on capital employed.

As an example, let us take a strata title home unit purchased for $155,000. By establishing its income and outgoings, we can arrive at a net return.

Purchase Price $155,000
Annual rental income @ $210.00 per week or $10,920 per annum

HOW TO CALCULATE OUTGOINGS

To determine profit, we must obtain and deduct all expected annual outgoings such as:

- Maintenance
- Property management
- Rates and repairs
- Body corporate levies
- Insurance
- Depreciation
- Vacancies

- Taxation (land tax if applicable)

Maintenance

All costs relating to the general upkeep, cleaning and replacement of items required to keep the property in good running order and suitably presented for tenants. Items that fall into this category include:

- Public lighting
- Cleaning of halls and stairs, laundries, lobbies, car parks and grounds
- Cleaning of apartments ready for new tenants
- Gardening and gardening materials
- Replacements
- Internal painting
- Plumbing repairs
- Electrical repairs

Management Costs

Management costs relate to the fees paid to a real estate company to lease the property, collect rents, keep records and arrange for and supervise staff and maintenance work.

Rates

In most areas there are two separate rating authorities:

Council rates: A rate levy assessed by the local government authority in the area in which the investment will be located and is assessed on the unimproved capital value of the land. A visit to the rating clerk at the local council chambers will give the exact rate figure.

Water Rates: Each region in Australia has its own water authority who will supply their cost structures but is usually based on a fixed minimum charge for water plus a set rate per kilolitre of water used. Sewerage is also usually a fixed charge

Insurance

An insurance policy is required to cover fire, contents, burglary, glass, storm, and tempest damage. A public liability coverage is also necessary. Loss of rent is also worth considering. In strata titled property the owners corporation insures the building structure. An insurance broker or an underwriter can provide information on suitable cover and premium costs.

Depreciation – Prime Cost and Written Down

Depreciation is the allowance claimed for the loss in value of an asset through wear and tear and obsolescence.

The estimate for this allowance is arrived at as follows:

$$\frac{\text{Cost Price of asset}}{\text{No. of years of useful life}} = \text{Annual rate of depreciation}$$

For example:

A carpet costs $3000 and its useful life is expected to be four years. Therefore, the amount which may be written off each year would be $750 so that at the end of the four-year period the book value of the carpet would be nil.

Taxpayers are at liberty to make any reasonable estimate of the useful life of an asset for internal accounting purposes but the ATO does have defined schedules of depreciation rates on various items.

The taxpayer may use one of two methods to calculate depreciation - the prime cost method or diminishing value method.

Prime Cost Method

Cost price x percentage rate of depreciation = annual allowance

For example, carpets:

Cost price	$3,000
Rate allowed under Prime Cost Method	17%
Allowance claimable	$510 per annum

Diminishing Value Method

Opening or written down value x percentage rate of depreciation

For example, carpets:

1st Year	Opening Value	$3,000
	Rate allowed under Diminishing Value Method	25%
	Allowance claimed 1st year	$750
2nd Year	Written down value ($3,000 - $750)	$2,250
	Rate allowed	25%
	Allowance claimable	$562
3rd Year	Written down value ($2,250 - $562)	$1,688
	Rate allowed	25%
	Allowance claimable	$422

As a quick reference, here are typical examples of allowances claimable as deductions by the Taxation Department. Some of the most commonly applied rates in residential investment are listed below.

ITEM	PRIME COST	DIMISHING VALUE
Carpets	17%	25%
Blinds	13%	20%
Clothes Dryer	20%	30%
Electric Lifts	13%	20%
Air Conditioning (depending on type)	7 - 17%	10 - 25%
Furniture & Fittings	13%	20%
Hot Water Systems	13%	20%
Microwave Oven	20%	30%
Stoves	13%	20%

Property investors will usually apply the Diminishing Value method as it effectively pulls forward much of the benefits into the early years when cash flow is most sensitive.

Body Corporate Levies

There are two amounts levied under the Strata Titles Act. They are the administration fund and the sinking fund.

The Administration Fund

This fund is levied by the appointed Owners Corporation manager to cover costs that include:

- Bank charges
- Cleaning of common areas
- Gardening
- Common electricity
- Insurance - building, public liability
- Maintenance
- Replacements
- Rubbish removal

- Body corporate management fees
- Common property rates
- Replacement of paths, fencing, paving
- Audit fees
- Miscellaneous expenses

Sinking Fund

This is levied to create a fund over time to cover future major maintenance and capital costs that may include:

- Painting
- Replacement of guttering, fences
- Driveways
- Other major structural faults or replacements

An estimate is made by the Owners Corporation of the future cost of these items and a fund created and built up over time to meet these costs as they occur.

Land Tax

This is a state tax applicable in most Australian states. Rates may vary from year to year and from state to state.

For instance, in New South Wales in 2021, the tax is assessed on the unimproved capital value of the land over a threshold figure of $755,000. The principal place of residence is exempt. Land tax is an expense and is tax deductible.

Most investors in medium density property can own 5 or 6 moderately valued investment properties before they start to incur land tax.

Contents Insurance

This is often part of a landlord protection policy which will also cover loss of rent in some situations and malicious damage. An estimate can be obtained from insurance companies or brokers of the total premium payable for the cover required.

Building Depreciation

This subject is dealt with elsewhere but is not generally regarded as a cost against income in establishing a net return or yield.

It is a tax concession rather than an operating cost. The net yield on property is a before tax return whereas building depreciation is a deduction for income tax purposes and would be applied when establishing an after-tax return.

Vacancy

Some research will need to be done to establish the vacancy rate in the locality. There are sources online who publish vacancy rates by suburb and region.

Unless something indicates otherwise, we find a vacancy estimate of 2% is adequate. You may have the same tenant for a few years with obviously no vacancy during that period. Conversely you may have a few tenants in a short period with vacancies between each one. It tends to average out over time.

With all the outgoings tabulated, we can now prepare a Net Profit and Loss Report. These figures are estimated by way of example and will vary from property to property.

Purchase Price		$155,000
Rental Income @ $210 per week		$10,920
Outgoings:	Council Rates	$435
	Water Rates	$365
	Body Corporate Levies	$880
	Insurance	$220
	Repairs & Maintenance	$100
	Depreciation Fixtures & Fittings	$1,200
	Management Fees	$728
	Letting Fee	$210
	Vacancy	$208
	Land Tax Single Holding	NIL
Total Outgoings		$4,346
Net Annual Income		$6,574

The profit and loss statement shows a net return of $6,574, after meeting all expenses, on the purchase price of $155,000. That is the profit that can be earned if one outlays in cash the amount required to purchase the investment.

Years Purchase and Yield

To make comparison against other relative investments, it is necessary to express the profit as a percentage of outlay.

$$\frac{\text{Purchase Price}}{\text{Net Profit}} = \text{Years purchase}$$

Years purchase then represents the number of years, at that level of profit, that would be required to return the original capital outlay.

$$\frac{\$155{,}000}{\$6{,}574} = 23.57 \text{ Years purchase}$$

At an annual profit rate of $6,574 it would take 23.57 years to return the original capital of $155,000. We can now express that as a percentage by dividing the years purchase into 100.

$$\frac{100}{23.57} = 4.24\%$$

The equation to establish a percentage return can be reduced to the simple form:

Net profit / Purchase price expressed as a percentage
$6,574 / $155,000. = 4.24%

The above equation does not take into account building depreciation allowances nor the effects of leverage, interest expense deductions, or after-tax returns, but does demonstrate in its simplest form the formula to be applied in establishing a net yield. It also allows for comparison of income return between properties and with other forms of investment.

Chapter 10

CAPITAL GROWTH - THE NUMBER ONE CONSIDERATION

Over the years we have seen many misconceptions about investing in property.

THE MOST COMMON MISCONCEPTIONS

The most common misconceptions about property investment, and these leave all others behind by a country mile, would be firstly, that you need to have a high income or large amount of cash to invest in property. We have already seen in earlier chapters that this is simply not the case and even more so in recent times with interest rates at lifetime lows.

Another one is where people confuse the desirability of a property with its likely future performance. By that we mean the tendency to believe that an upscale, aesthetically pleasing, exotically located property will outperform its more average counterpart because its desirability means more people want it, which will in turn drive its rental and capital value.

All these notions could not be further from the truth.

It is understandable though. Typically, people looking to invest in property without the wisdom of their own or somebody else's personal experience do not have much to go on. Even now sources of reliable property investment information are actually few and far between. Most of the information out there is targeting home buyers not investors.

Consequently, in such an information vacuum, it is natural enough to rely heavily on whatever information may be available, however scant it may be. The danger is that this can lead to over-emphasising the relevance or importance of some of this information.

THE MOST ASKED QUESTION

Probably the most common question asked of real estate agents by investors is "how much rent could we get for this property?"

A fair enough question, and one of the pieces of information we need to know to assess the merits of a particular property. Almost as important are the expenses that we pay out of the rent we receive all of which are detailed in the previous chapter.

The problem is it is all too easy to focus too heavily on the rental income which can be problematic in that it distracts us from the reason we are investing in the first place - to build wealth or net worth through the increasing value of our property investments - capital growth.

Certainly, this is true for anybody that substantially borrows to purchase property, especially if negatively geared.

SUBSIDISING THE COST

Someone who borrows enough of the purchase price of the property that the after tax annual cost of holding the property is a negative amount, is negatively geared. This means they are subsidising the ongoing cost. It is costing them money, usually a relatively low amount but, nevertheless it is a cost.

Therefore, if we are subsidising the cost of the investment there must be a reward. That reward is the capital growth over time.

It matters less how much rent we receive if our primary reward is the growth in value. The difference between high and modest rent will not have a dramatic effect on the ongoing holding cost, whereas the difference between strong and ordinary growth will have a massive effect on the result over time.

It must follow that growth is the number one consideration in the whole property investment equation.

In fact, there is a correlation between rent and growth which further underlines the point. At least in general terms, it is usually the case that the higher the rental or income yield, the lower the growth expectation and vice versa.

For example, if rental income were the most important consideration, we would all go to an old, run down, out of favour part of town and buy small industrial units where we could get the highest possible rental yield. But would we achieve the capital growth, for that matter would we in fact find or consistently keep a tenant?

If we did not expect the growth to occur, then it simply would not serve to achieve our objective of growing net worth.

A similar and related issue is the popularity of "negative gearing" as an end in itself. Many organisations and even some media commentators promote the benefits of negative gearing as if nothing else matters.

As we have already discussed, if the investment is costing us money, no matter how small that amount might be, it is still a cost. We do it for the capital growth. As wonderful as the taxation advantages can be in helping to keep the cost of holding property to low levels, no amount of tax advantage can in itself build wealth. Only the capital growth over time can help us achieve that.

Besides the risk of overestimating the value of a high rental, or getting carried away on the negative gearing bandwagon, the overwhelming dominance of capital growth as the number one consideration in building wealth through property investment is paramount.

If you are NOT convinced that capital growth is going to occur in the future, do not negatively gear and possibly do not invest in property at all.

Chapter 11

ALWAYS BUY - NEVER SELL

In previous books we have strongly advocated the principle "Always Buy Never Sell". Nothing has changed our view.

How often we see investors enter the property market and as soon as the going gets a little tough they sell out, sometimes losing money. Alternatively, they may, after modest gains in value, choose to sell believing this to be the only way to realise a profit.

There are many reasons why some investors do not persevere with the circumstances that prevail.

WHY DO INVESTORS SELL AT THE WRONG TIME?

Purchasing property at the peak of the market is one of the reasons that may cause investors to lose their nerve and sell. Taking on more debt than is safe and comfortable under all circumstances is another one.

There are many reasons why an investor may choose to sell and exit the market. One of the most common is impatience. We mentioned time, information, and patience earlier.

If the property has not performed well within the first few years, and all the investor is experiencing is the outlaying of property expenses and making loan payments, fatigue may set in and the decision to sell is made, even though the market is weak. The most likely reason the property has not performed well is it was acquired at the wrong time in the property cycle, probably during the last boom close to the price peak.

The answer to the question "why do investors sell at the wrong time", is usually because they bought at the wrong time.

THE PROPERTY CLOCK

If an investor purchases at a high point in the cycle they may need to wait for the top of the next cycle to show a satisfactory gain that approximates the long-term rate of growth. Over the last four cycles in Sydney that has been anything from eight to fifteen years.

Referring to the chapter entitled "A Simple Philosophy", we advocate buying when the market is down and selling, if necessary, when the market is up. A counter-cyclical strategy.

THE INVESTMENT WINDOW

Buying during the period before the market commences a major growth phase is the objective. That window of opportunity could stretch out over as much as three or four years. Nobody really knows in advance what day the market will turn, but market forces such as rental vacancies, rates of construction, affordability and underlying demand provide trends that indicate when the investment window is opening.

TIME MAXIMISES GROWTH

We have been discussing timing, but time itself is the real secret to successful property investment. Property purchased even at a time that does not maximise growth potential, provided it is well selected for design, location, and type, is properly and conservatively financed, and held over the long term, will still likely exceed the performance of other forms of investment.

Property held over the long term will continue to provide security for those who embark on a concentrated program of property investment, especially if they keep adding to their portfolio.

Poor timing can contribute to a lessor growth factor but time itself will help correct mistakes. The worst mistake may be not to buy any residential property at all. That may actually be the second worst mistake you can make – it is only an opportunity cost. The worst is buying at the top of the market, getting impatient and selling a few years later in the slump. Then you would most likely suffer actual capital loss and have a bruised investment psyche that puts you off property investment for life. It happens all the time.

Embracing the concept of "Always Buy Never Sell" serves to focus our attention on the long term and avoid the mistakes of the impatient investor.

THE STORY OF ONE INVESTOR WHO NEVER SOLD

In the mid 70's a client of Fred's, we will call him David, asked him to locate a particular investment opportunity. David a successful lawyer who believed in the virtues of property investment. He realised the day would come when he would have to step down from his senior position and would probably retire in about twenty years to pursue other activities.

The brief was to locate property that would show exceptional growth over the following twenty years providing, in effect, a personal superannuation fund for David. It did not need to be income producing as David's income over the next twenty years would be more than adequate for his needs. Fred was not too happy about the non-income producing aspect of the brief. After all it was ingrained in his philosophy that all property investment should be income producing to take advantage of loan interest deductibility, depreciation etc. But David did not intend to use borrowed funds. This was an exercise in sheer growth accumulation over a long period.

USING GOVERNMENT PLANNING

At that time, the New South Wales Government had released "The Sydney Regional Outline Plan". A document that designated, regions of Sydney to be rezoned from rural to residential, catering for Sydney's future housing needs to the year 2000.

Although specific land titles or areas were not designated, close scrutiny and research identified areas that seemed reasonably certain to be included in future rezoning as Sydney expanded.

The D F Johnson companies at that time had secured several such properties for its clients in syndicated groups.

Fred recommended to David that he acquire one of these sites in his own right. He paid $65,000 for 8 acres of land in what was then the western outskirts of the city.

Many of the syndicated groups sold their properties at various stages realising excellent profits. Even where the land had not been released for rezoning, the elapsed time since acquisition had shortened the time before future release would probably occur, thus enhancing its value.

David did not sell. No doubt he was tempted on many occasions with some lucrative offers coming his way over the years. His successful career continued, but in 1992 David decided to retire. Around that time his land was promulgated for rezoning. David entered into serious negotiations with statutory authorities to determine town planning considerations as well as the supply of utilities to the site and to resolve environmental matters. These negotiations continued for some years until one day in 1995, Fred, now also retired, received a phone call from David to say he was coming to see him. He arrived carrying a dozen bottles of top shelf champagne to celebrate the approval of subdivision of the land into 100 housing lots, giving the land a retail value of about $13 million.

Foresight, perseverance and stickability had paid off for David who had been carrying holding costs and out of pocket expenses for over twenty years.

He could have sold many times over, but he hung in and reaped the rewards.

Fred has helped many thousands of investors to real estate wealth, some to large fortunes. Many have written to him to show their appreciation. David was the only one to show up with a crate of champagne.

This is an extraordinary story. But it emphasises the principal. Always buy and never sell.

ANOTHER HAPPY HISTORY

Fred's first book "How to Get Real Estate Rich" was published in 1969. It was a best seller. It was the first book ever published in Australia by an Australian author that dealt specifically with investment in real estate in Australia. Many North American books had been written on the subject, but they were not entirely applicable to Australian conditions.

In that book he related the story of Hugh and Ann Bennett who used equity in their home, purchased years previously, to acquire land and develop twenty-four rental apartments to hold for long term income and growth.

They used the equity in their home plus $6000 cash. The total cost of the development, including the land, was $178,400.

Is it almost unbelievable, twenty-four apartments for only $178,400, but that was in the late sixties.

On completion of building the construction loan was converted to an interest only loan for ten years at a fixed interest rate.

HOW $6,000 GREW INTO A FORTUNE

Overall, the Bennett's had invested $6,000 cash in the project, the borrowings coming from their home and the newly constructed property.

Fred points out in that example that Hugh and Ann were fictitious persons, but the facts were true. He now reveals that the property was acquired and developed by his own family group.

Although time has seen some of the apartments pass to other family members and estate beneficiaries the performance of this property can easily be traced from its construction in 1968 to today.

Fred is now in his late eighties. It is only in recent years he has chosen to divest himself of the remaining apartments which he continued to hold for almost fifty years.

The apartments in that building are currently worth around $600,000 each taking the total value of the building of 24 units to over $14 million.

HOW DO YOU REALISE A PROFIT IF YOU DO NOT SELL?

The answer is technically you cannot. You only realise a profit when you sell. You also only incur capital gains tax when you realise a profit by sale. The accumulation of wealth through property ownership creates a capacity to borrow and a capital nest egg for cash flow in the future when income from personal exertion ceases.

HOW TO ENHANCE LIFESTYLE

With a large equity in property, one would hope to be able to enjoy an improved lifestyle. Whatever that lifestyle means to you.

Whether your income is derived from a business, the gig economy or as a salaried employee, additional cash may be required from time to time to fund lifestyle. With accumulated assets, one can always borrow to access cash for lifestyle purposes even though it may not be a tax-deductible expense. It may be more productive to borrow against the increased value of your properties rather than selling which cuts off any future growth from the property and triggers tax liabilities.

When personal income stops, perhaps in retirement, a portion of the property portfolio could be sold to reduce borrowings and increase net income for living expenses. When further capital is required more property can be sold. Is this breaking our rule of "Always Buy Never Sell"? Yes, it is, but after years of holding property that has substantially increased in value, maintaining a high standard of living is a reasonable conclusion to a lifetime of property accumulation.

Chapter 12

WILL PROPERTY VALUES KEEP RISING?

It is easy to look back on previous price charts and see how real estate values have increased over time.

Impressive as it has been, it has also been gradual in time span. It is not a thing people are noticing and actively thinking about day to day and certainly few people keep such records. For most, the family home is the main point of reference and even then, few have its value updated on a regular basis, although a sale down the street often provides an indication. We know what we paid for our home and, if we have lived in it for several years, we probably stay in touch with the market to some extent.

THE NEXT 50 YEARS OF GROWTH

Historical growth is one thing. Prices look cheap in hindsight. What is harder to accept is, if we project the same rate of growth into the future the numbers become staggering.

The Sydney median house price fifty years ago, in 1970, was $18,500. The median in June 2020 was $1,103,100. That is a growth rate of 8.5%.

If we project the median Sydney house price forward by 50 years at 8.5% annual growth it takes the median Sydney house to $65,300,000.

Such a figure seems incomprehensible – but it is just mathematics.

If we tone it down a bit and just project forward fifteen years, the median house grows to $3,750,000. More credible – but the same mathematics.

Can values really keep rising at that rate? Surely as soon as I purchase all the rules will change. Maybe they will, but if the historical evidence is not enough let us look at the practical and demographic evidence.

Property values are driven by the supply demand equation which we have already well canvassed. How then can the growth equation be proved by its separate elements?

DEMOGRAPHICS DRIVE DEMAND

Population growth is an essential element. This country is huge in area and low in population. Twenty-six million people in the same land area as the United States where the population is 330 million.

In Australia, our population growth rates have been falling for a few years reflecting a decline in net overseas migration. The rate of births or natural increase has been very consistent.

If the Australian population went into a long decline that would be a problem. Governments continue to encourage the birth rate with tax incentives and other benefits, while immigration rises and falls with the economic cycle, political ideology and, as it turns out, worldwide health pandemics.

There are headwinds ahead. The fall-off in immigration during the pandemic will have an impact on all markets, including residential property for a while. Government will no doubt do everything in its power to boost immigration numbers over the next few years.

New household formation continues and the number of people approaching the important first homebuyer age group is looking healthy.

BABY BOOMERS

We cannot discuss population without mentioning the baby boomers - a phenomenon of the last seventy-five years. The children of the post-World War II period. The youngest boomers are currently turning sixty while those older than 75 are not technically boomers. They are unimaginatively called pre-boomers.

Remember we noted the current tightness of regional markets in New South Wales? And that it really started when the market was peaking back in 2017? Gone are the days when parents moved in with the kids or into the granny flat. Now they retire to the beach or quaint country towns.

SUPPLY - THE OTHER HALF OF THE EQUATION

The rate of construction or supply of new housing moves up and down with demand. The market has great difficulty balancing the two. It is like trying to stop an ocean liner in mid ocean. When demand subsides, it takes construction a long time to apply the brakes effectively. We have previously discussed how, with some reasonable accuracy, this aspect of supply can be predicted, but there are other aspects of supply that are also noteworthy.

LIMITED LAND SUPPLY

Geographically some areas are more subject to supply constraints than others. The best example of this is Sydney, a city of limited land supply. Being a coastal town, it can only expand north, south and west. But to the west the Great Dividing Range prevents expansion beyond Penrith. To the South, the Royal National Park and Sydney's water catchment areas, and to the north, the rugged Hawkesbury Valley and national parks prevent expansion. It is a land-locked city. As time passes the availability of serviceable land reduces. Harbour, beach, river, and parkland areas achieve premium values.

Other areas have land shortages and supply limitations too. The Gold Coast, Noosa Heads and Canberra are examples although not to the extent of Sydney.

Combine Sydney's land constraints with a growing population approaching five million and it is not difficult to conclude that Sydney looms as the best bet for future growth above other locations around the nation.

But we should not lose track of what we are discussing here. Will property values keep rising?

Some places will fare better than others, but we believe residential values will continue to rise, in the usual cyclical fashion, throughout Australia, into the foreseeable future.

We do not believe the growth rates of the past will continue. And they do not need to. With a low inflation environment likely to continue for some time, if you are attracting capital growth at even half the rate of the past it is still an exceptional result.

If we project the current Sydney median house price forward at just 4.5% per annum, in fifteen years it is $2,135,000. In 50 years, it would be $9,950,000.

Chapter 13

DOES LOW INFLATION MEAN LOW GROWTH?

In recent years, during which we have seen inflation falling to low levels, a view has emerged that low inflation means low, or no growth in property values.

As we have discussed, there is a link between growth rates and inflation, but it is not necessarily a negative at all. There are many benefits from investing in property in a low inflation environment, and particular risks in investing in a high inflation environment.

The key to understanding the relationship between inflation and capital growth, is found in two factors in particular.

Firstly, as discussed earlier, the real benefit from capital growth is maintaining a hedge against inflation, and over and above that, increasing the purchasing power of capital by having it increase in value ahead of the rate of inflation. Any change in value for a given period above or below the rate of inflation is called the "real" growth rate.

We know that historically Sydney house prices have increased over the long term at around 9% per annum compound. Inflation during the same period has averaged around 6.5% per annum. This means the "real" rate of growth, that is, the growth above the inflation rate, which is increasing the purchasing power of our capital, and therefore our "real" wealth, has averaged around 2.5% per annum.

If house prices increased by 15%, the media would be telling us the market was booming. If, at the same time inflation was 12.5%, not that we are likely to return to that anytime soon, it translates to a real increase of 2.5%. More akin to the long-term growth rate than a boom.

Why then, when inflation is 2.5%, and values increase 5%, again giving us a 2.5% real increase, do they not see it? In real purchasing power terms, the result is virtually the same.

It could be that "real" growth rates are unfamiliar and unless we see large "nominal" or face value increases, we perceive that not much is happening on the growth front.

But that is not necessarily so.

THE INVISIBLE BOOM

The 1994 year is a good example. The Sydney median house price increased during that year by around 12%. Inflation was around 2%. Therefore the "real" increase was about 10% above the rate of inflation. Five times the rate of inflation itself, and equal to around four years of long-term real growth. It was a low inflation mini boom that nobody noticed. It certainly did not make headlines at the time.

A growth rate in any year of 10% above inflation is an excellent result in anyone's language, irrespective of whether inflation is high or low. In fact, in real terms even though it was not part of a longer sustained upturn, 1994 was the third strongest year of real growth Sydney had experienced in the almost 15 years leading up to that point in time.

The second key to understanding the role of inflation on residential property values is found in analysing the actual source of capital growth.

It is an obvious truth that inflation has an impact on construction costs, in particular on building materials and labour. This is the point from which conventional wisdom construes that if building replacement costs rise, then values will rise. But the main point is missed.

LAND DELIVERS GROWTH

It is land which generates and delivers most of the capital growth we experience in property ownership. Land is the finite commodity most effected by the forces of supply and demand, discussed in earlier chapters. Buildings depreciate, or fall in value, until one day, when the bulldozer arrives, they have virtually no value. Land values are not directly driven by inflation.

Historically, we have seen many examples of housing markets around Australia performing and reacting quite differently to economic forces including inflation.

The economic recession of the early nineties was a turning point for inflation. Until then inflation had been over 7% and often over 10% for almost twenty years. During that recession values in most cities remained static as significant shortages of property did not exist to support growth. In contrast, the Canberra market, where release of new land was an ordered process controlled by the National Capital Development Commission, saw an increase in values of over 30% in that two-year period. There was a shortage of land. Property value growth was strong despite inflation plummeting and economic recession during that period. The shortage of land was a stronger force, and it defies the notion that low inflation leads to low growth.

There will always be pundits who will point to economic factors, such as low inflation leading to low wages growth, which in turn restrains housing affordability and limits capital growth.

The good example to counter these arguments is the experience of the mid to late eighties, where under the "Accord" with the ACTU, wages generally grew at less than the rate of inflation, but Sydney experienced the strongest boom it had witnessed in decades.

LOW INFLATION - LOW RISK

If the golden rule of investment and creating sustainable real wealth is not "how to make the most", but "how to lose the least", then there is in fact a real positive in holding residential property for investment purposes in a low inflation environment - less downside risk. There have been many periods where values are not rising and inflation has been high, contradicting the idea that high inflation leads to strong growth. In real terms during such periods, we are losing money or at least the purchasing power of our capital is diminished as inflation erodes its value.

Between 1981 and 1987, a very flat period in the Sydney market, real property prices fell by over 25%, even though the market appeared to be making marginal gains each year. Such was the effect of high inflation.

On balance a modest level of inflation may be desirable if for no other reason than to grease the wheels of market psychology. More importantly, one should beware the conventional wisdom, remembering that most people buy property at the top of the boom. The majority are often wrong.

Chapter 14

SELECTING THE BEST PROPERTY

Of 1.85 million residential dwellings in Sydney over 500,000 are owned by investors. We like to think the majority of those were acquired to generate capital growth and rental income for all the right strategic reasons. The reality is that a large proportion of rental properties are owned by accidental investors. People who have rented out property inherited from family, workers on secondment renting out their house while they are away, people trapped overseas during a pandemic, grey nomads renting out the family home while on the road, or other life and lifestyle reasons.

The value of all residential investment property in Sydney is around $450 billion. Total rent payable on these properties is estimated at over $18 billion per annum. A huge market, involving massive amounts of capital and resources.

Why is so little serious attention given to residential property investment in the media. The renovation shows on television do not talk about investment principles. The newspaper columns on residential property tend to focus on high value "trophy" properties and their celebrity owners. And most of the businesses promoting property investment seem to think anytime is a good time to buy when clearly it is not.

Paradoxically, the reason for a lack of quality residential investment information is also of residential property's main advantages. The market is not dominated by investors.

As we have discussed, around 65% of the residential market is comprised of people owning or paying off their own homes. As investors, this is our secret ingredient. The majority of those in the market in which we invest do not act according to normal investment criteria or motivation. If times get tough the majority of those homeowners do not panic and rush to sell as can happen in virtually every other medium where we invest our hard-earned funds. It is a benefit of residential investment which is unique.

Pandering to the needs and desires of the aspirational homebuyer market is the main game because those people are the main audience.

Consequently, the qualities to look for in a good investment property can be overlooked or glossed over with the well-worn adage of location, location, location. It is not that simple. When assessing the worthiness of a property for investment purposes, there are many things to consider.

THE KEY POINTS

Design and Utility

Fifty years ago, home units were specifically built for the rental market and were called flats. The flats of yesteryear are typically on the small side, of basic design and often with open car spaces and shared laundries. Times change. These days many people choose medium density accommodation as a first preference. These are people with busy lifestyles who do not want lawns to mow or houses to maintain.

With 65% of the market being homeowners, and perhaps a quarter of the market preferring medium density accommodation, developers concluded during the eighties that it might be a good idea to design and build dwellings which met this market demand.

Typically, a new apartment today is 25% larger than its predecessors, includes security systems, ensuite bathrooms, defined entry lobbies, lock up garages, larger balconies or courtyards, intensive landscaping and often recreational facilities of some sort.

The old school notion that one kind of design worked for investors and their tenants while another more generous version suited owner-occupiers has gone. And a good thing too.

If the bulk of demand in the residential market comes from owner-occupiers, investing in property that is not attractive to those people would not be a good idea.

Finance

The most critical aspect of finance is making the distinction between borrowing for home ownership and for investment purposes.

When buying a home, a principal and interest loan, often at a variable rate, which we seek to reduce as quickly as possible, is usually the right approach. Using this type of borrowing for investment reduces the financial efficiency of the investment dramatically. When we use our available cash flow to reduce the principal on an investment property loan two things happen.

Firstly, the overall tax saving we enjoy, and which allows us to hold property at relatively low cost starts to diminish. Secondly, the same funds we are using to reduce principal, could potentially be used to own and subsidise a second investment property, thereby increasing potential capital growth.

The golden rules of investment include two important points, protecting what we already have, and minimising risk by knowing as much as possible in advance, thereby avoiding future surprises.

In finance terms this means keeping borrowings to overall comfortable levels and locking finance into fixed term, fixed rate, interest only loans. Right now, interest rates are the lowest of our lifetimes and fixing the rate may not be as mission critical as in the past, however we still advocate interest only borrowing for cashflow efficiency and portfolio growth.

Building Allowance

Every residential property in Australia which commenced construction after 17 July 1985, and is held as an investment, qualifies for an annual tax deductible allowance of 2.5% of the original construction cost of the improvements on the land.

For example, a new $500,000 property purchased today may have cost $250,000 to build with the balance being the land value and development profit. A building allowance of 2.5% would generate a tax deduction of $6,250 a year for forty years.

It is rare, but we once found a property where the original construction cost exceeded the purchase price. The original developer had chronically overcapitalised in a falling market. The annual building allowance this generated turned an average investment into an extraordinary investment.

Value

Considerable capital gain can be achieved at point of purchase. Buying at less than market value translates into capital gain. However, saying it and doing it can be entirely different matters. No vendor sets out to sell property at a bargain price.

Bargains do appear for a variety of reasons. Forced sales through financial stress or family issues account for the major proportion of so-called bargains.

But a bargain is sometimes more perceived than real. We have had situations where an investor has told us of a great deal they made on a purchase, how they negotiated hard to achieve a below market price, only to be told by the vendor of the same property what a great price they got. What is a bargain for one is often a killing to another.

One of our investment criteria is to ensure that the price we buy or sell for is fair. To constantly hunt for a bargain is often not to buy at all, and to always maximise selling price often means remaining the owner.

If throughout your lifetime you bought and sold every property at fair value, you would have little to complain about. The objective then is to be sure that the consideration paid or received represents fair market value.

The simple definition of market value is the price that would be paid for a property, when exposed to the open market for a reasonable time, by an informed purchaser assuming both parties are willing but not anxious.

Arriving at market value is the task of an expert, and a qualified valuer can be engaged for the purpose. If borrowings are required to complete the purchase the lender will usually have a valuation carried out, at your expense of course, and this will act as a safety net for the inexperienced purchaser. Just be aware the lender may instruct the valuer to estimate value "for mortgage purposes" which may be different to open market value.

During the process of inspecting property for sale, buyers are in fact using one of the most effective methods of residential property valuation - comparison. Identifying comparable sales in the local market is the mainstay of residential valuation. While inspecting lots of properties on the market provides good feel for prices, values are based on actual sales rather than asking prices. Sale prices are freely available online.

Rental Income

Producing sufficient rental income to service borrowings and/or provide a net yield is an important ingredient. Extensive research needs to be done to prove a rental value for the prospective investment property. Systematic analysis of other rental properties of a similar nature and location needs to be completed. While the amount of rental income may not be the most critical thing to consider in a growth investment, it is essential information to have to estimate before and after tax cashflows. You should know how much the investment will cost to hold. It is also useful for comparison with other prospective properties.

Borrowing Capacity

Every investor has a potential to borrow. Keeping those borrowings to manageable levels that also provide maximum returns and tax benefits requires special consideration. We have long advocated that investors would be wise from a risk management perspective to never use more than 75% of their ability to borrow at any point in time. To do that you need to know your maximum borrowing capacity. A good mortgage broker can be an excellent source of this information. Just be sure to ask them the specific question.

Capital Growth

It cannot be taken for granted that all property will grow in value in unison. Whilst it can be assumed that all properties in a specific geographic market will ultimately increase in value at consistent rates, there can be short term differences. Regard for growth potential as it impacts a specific property needs to be considered.

It is not possible to foresee all the pluses and minuses, but it is a good idea to know as much as possible about the local area as you can.

This requires extensive investigation into local transport, employment opportunities, public infrastructure and other available services as well as major development activity in the area that may enhance or detract from value growth in the future.

We have also noted over the years how some elements of a local market study can be a bit misleading. One is major infrastructure announcements, especially transport improvements. Things like very fast train services, wave-piercing ferries, new freeways, and road tunnels at face value sound like they may benefit a particular area but very often never materialise or take many years to complete. In our experience the positive impact of these sorts of things tends to be deferred until actual completion of the infrastructure project.

Inflation

In projecting future cashflows for any property an assumption must be made on the effect of inflation on costs and expenses. Even though inflation may be low today, if we are projecting cash flows over say a ten-year period, an average inflation rate for that future period must be assessed based on a reasonable view of likely future economic events.

Interest Rates

Interest rates impact total return. Like rental income, they are important although not the most important aspect of the investment decision. Remember interest payments for investment purposes are tax deductible. Minimising interest rates at time of purchase is important as the amount of loan interest has a substantial bearing on after tax cashflow. If you fix the interest rate you have removed the risk of nasty surprises, at least for a time. If you borrow at a variable rate you will be riding the roller-coaster no matter how attractive the rate is up-front.

Property Expenses

Accurately assessing the holding costs on property requires effort and experience. Carrying out calculations on the back of an envelope is not satisfactory. Guessing or approximating is not acceptable. All outgoings must be established and checked for correctness and none overlooked.

We have in an earlier chapter entitled "Establishing a Net Yield" outlined the process in assessing proper property expenses.

Depreciation on fixtures, fittings, and furnishings

Not to be confused with the building depreciation allowance already included in this check list, depreciation on these items can provide excellent tax benefits, especially in the early years of the investment. Where possible, the value of the items needs to be clearly established in advance in order to provide maximum benefits and an accurate after-tax cost.

After Tax Cashflow

Knowing how much an investment will cost to hold is intrinsic to appraisal of the property purchase decision. This is critical in negative gearing. Proper budgeting will prevent problems down the line.

An assessment of the after-tax cashflows from a specific property will require information on the property as well as the individual owner or prospective owner. The personal marginal tax-rate of the individual helps quantify the amount of tax saving and the after-tax cost, if any.

Internal Rate of Return

The internal rate of return is the profit from all sources, earned on capital invested, including purchase costs, over time. It takes into account meeting any cash shortfalls and is the only figure that reveals the total picture and should be accurately assessed. It is a complicated calculation which makes a computer spreadsheet or specialist program essential.

Purchase Costs

No investment analysis can be completed unless purchase costs are established. These include stamp duty, legal costs, lenders mortgage insurance, valuation fees, statutory charges, and total borrowing expenses.

Renovation Costs

Renovations carried out in certain time spans attract depreciation allowances, even though a building may not comply for depreciation because of its construction date. Any renovations since 17 July 1985 will provide depreciation benefits at rates relative to the date the renovations were commenced. Proper assessment of those costs needs to be established.

Rental Yield

There are two calculations necessary in determining rental yield. The gross yield is calculated by expressing the total annual rental income to purchase price as a percentage. Net yield means rental income less all operating costs expressed as a percentage of purchase price. Both those calculations are generally considered to be before any consideration of interest expenses, building allowance or purchase costs. This allows comparison between properties.

NOT TO BE TREATED LIGHTLY

Investment in property is not to be treated lightly. Large sums of money are usually involved in a property transaction and thorough research and assessment is imperative.

In any decision-making process you need all the available data first. A good decision requires good information. In fact, the decision can make itself if you are properly informed.

Chapter 15

OTHER TYPES OF INVESTMENT AND WHY TO AVOID THEM

"Don't put all your eggs in one basket" has become the investment catch-cry of the century. There is another school of investment thought which says, "Put all your eggs in one basket and watch the basket".

One of the great things about ownership of property as a means of creating and maintaining real wealth, is that the property remains totally under your control. The services of various professionals such as property managers, investment planners, financiers and lawyers are available to assist in dealing with property, but in the end the decisions are exclusively yours.

In contrast, other investment types, in particular those managed by large organisations, banks, insurance companies, trustee companies etc. takeover most of the decision-making process. In return you pay fees for these services. The question is - is it worth it?

The performance of some of these large superannuation and other managed funds over recent years has left many pondering that exact question. No doubt there will be periods in the future where these funds will perform strongly, and there will again be times when they are weak. That is the nature of markets and investment. Generally, however it seems to us there is a greater problem with that kind of investment.

THE REAL GAIN

Most managed funds have relatively complicated fee structures but one that is almost universal is the annual charge of a percentage of the total assets of the fund paid to the fund manager. This is in addition to the running costs of the fund itself. Whilst these annual fees have fallen in recent years, they remain relatively high at around 1% to 1.5% of the value of the fund's assets.

If a property or share trust had total funds of say $100 million and the annual management fee was 1.5% of the value of the fund, then the manager would receive $1.5 million each year, in addition to various reimbursements and perhaps a range of other fees as well. This may appear fair and reasonable given the resources required to manage that amount of money safely and successfully on behalf of possibly thousands of small investors.

The problem lies in the fact that growth investments really serve two purposes. One is as a hedge against inflation in that the value of the investment rises at least in line with inflation and therefore the purchasing power of the capital is maintained. The other is creating additional wealth whereby the capital grows in value ahead of the rate of inflation and so the purchasing power of the capital increases. The real rate of return.

Most assets which rise in value over time, and there are really only two, shares and property, tend to average long term growth rates of 2% to 3% above the rate of inflation. If the fund manager receives say 1.5% of the value of the fund each year, then possibly more than half of the real gain over and above inflation is being used up in providing management. So, we are constantly behind the eight ball. If a fund manager is skilful enough to generate an investment performance that is consistently ahead of the market in which it is invested, then perhaps no problem. But history tells us that is not often the case.

Some would say managed investments serve a worthy purpose in giving investors without large resources access to the markets of the big players. By joining forces and employing a professional manager to make all the decisions and take care of the paperwork we can play in the big leagues.

And yes, that is probably true. But it also means these funds are designed to meet the needs of as many people as possible and are therefore designed for the average investor. Unfortunately, this can also translate to average performance. There are specialist funds available for specific situations but even in those funds the management fee, which is often higher in a specialist fund, continues to erode the real gain and therefore inhibits the ability to build real wealth.

STAYING IN CONTROL

This problem is not anybody's fault. The fund managers are providing a service and deserve to be paid. The real issue is why would you, as an investor with the forethought and motivation to read books on investment, place your money in a situation where the odds are inherently stacked against you. Especially when there are viable alternatives available which leave you in control of your own destiny and the maximum amount of the real gain is benefiting you by adding to your net worth.

Obviously, the alternative is investment in direct ownership of income producing property which will grow in value over time.

DIVERSIFICATION

The whole concept of diversification is based around minimising risk by exposing your money to a range of investment alternatives. In theory, if you invest in the three main asset classes, property, equities (shares) and fixed interest investments, you will be taking less risk by evening out the highs and lows which are a natural part of investment markets. This makes sense. It is what happens next that causes us concern.

Let us say you have $100,000 in cash and decide to see a financial planner to obtain advice on how to invest your cash for maximum return whilst keeping risk to manageable levels.

Your adviser talks about "diversification" and perhaps uses phrases like "modern portfolio theory", "risk/reward relationships", and "re-weighting". It is agreed that your $100,000 should be invested as follows:

Property	$35,000	33.2%
Shares	$28,000	26.5%
Fixed Interest	$32,500	30.8%
Cash	$10,000	9.4%
Total	$105,500	100%

The investments are duly made. The portfolio is diversified in keeping with "modern portfolio theory" and your adviser suggests meeting again in twelve months' time to review the portfolio and re-weight the investments if necessary. This is where the problem starts.

In twelve months, the value of the investments has changed in keeping with the respective market's performance during that time:

Property (trusts or listed companies)	$30,000	30%
Shares (direct ownership or trusts)	$30,000	30%
Fixed Interest Securities	$30,000	30%
Cash (cash management trusts)	$10,000	10%
Total	$100,000	100%

The total value of the portfolio has increased. In that particular year property increased in value, shares fell a little, the value of fixed interest investments rose due to a fall in interest rates (the capital value of bonds and similar securities can rise and fall) and the cash remained the same.

Your adviser now recommends making some changes to the portfolio to re-weight the investments back to the original percentage allocation. In other words, to bring property back to 30% by disposing of part of the property holding, using the proceeds to increase shares to 30% and cashing in some bonds to build up the cash reserves.

Proponents of this approach would argue that selling some property when that market has been rising to buy more shares when that market is down makes sense. And it does. But there are a couple of problems with this.

LIQUIDITY

Firstly, property is not a liquid investment, meaning you can not necessarily sell a few thousand dollars' worth of your property. This leads many in the investment community to consider only property trusts or companies that are listed on the stock exchange as a vehicle for property exposure. This raises the question of whether that investment is really a property investment or a share investment. It would certainly be subject to the market forces at work in the share market generally, as well as the underlying forces in the property market.

Secondly, with constant re-weighting of an investment portfolio, it means to some extent we are making investments which may well be sold in the short term, especially if they have performed well. This goes against the fundamental principles outlined in this book and proven over time by successful property investors - "always buy, never sell," the principle of accumulating a portfolio of property over time. This has become even more important since the introduction of Capital Gains Tax in 1985, which taxes only realised gains, that is only when and if an asset is sold.

This is not to say there is no value in diversification - there is. But rather than constantly playing with the mix of investments, we advocate that any amount an investor allocates to property investment out of total resources should then be separated and isolated from other investments and viewed as a planned program of building property wealth. Only this way can the full long-term benefits of compounding values be properly exploited.

Additionally, it is often the case that property investors will borrow part or all of the purchase price of a property and therefore not use their own capital as part of the purchase. The ability to do this creates the leverage discussed elsewhere in this book, which allows us to hold more property and receive more growth through the prudent use of borrowings. Whilst this clearly makes the concept of re-weighting an investment portfolio cumbersome and inappropriate, at least as it relates to property, it also highlights a disadvantage of other forms of investment.

LEVERAGE

We can borrow significant sums of money at relatively low cost to purchase income producing property held for investment purposes because residential property is regarded as the safest, and least volatile form of growth investment available.

Most banks will lend at least 80% of the value of a property, without mortgage insurance or other protection, because they perceive their money to be secure. This is not the case with other forms of investment. Yes, you can borrow money to buy shares. It will be more expensive, and the restrictions will be more severe including the possibility of "margin calls" which is where the lender can request a further input of capital if the shares fall substantially in value.

Without sounding too dramatic, lying awake at night hoping Wall Street does not affect the Australian market, which in turn causes your lender to call looking for funds to bring their lending percentage back into line, is not necessarily a comfortable position. To overcome this, you borrow less, and consequently own fewer shares and receive less benefit. Your ability to leverage your investment result is limited.

The ability to borrow to create leverage in other growth investments like gold bullion, commodities, antiques, stamps, businesses, precious gems, patents, and the like is restricted by the fact that lenders do not regard those investment types to be as secure as bricks and mortar. Many of them do not generate income and the increase in value over time is nowhere near as reliable or predictable as property has been over the long term.

Residential property has always been, and we believe will always be, the investment type which provides the best prospects to build real wealth by using the leverage of borrowings without venturing into the murky waters of other markets.

Chapter 16

BUT COULD I LIVE IN IT?

Deciding what and where to buy is one of the dilemmas facing property investors.

The options are wide and varied but there are well-worn paths. And as we have been saying, the well-worn paths do not always lead to investment success. Here are a few things to be aware of in starting to think about property in different locations.

LIFESTYLE

People with an interest in real estate often find themselves browsing real estate windows when on vacation.

The idea of a luxury apartment overlooking a beach or a rustic cottage with a few acres can be appealing - no one would deny that. The thought behind the interest usually centres on the possibility of personal use, pride of ownership and similar emotions rather than investment criteria. Many have gone broke harbouring such thoughts.

We will cover this in more detail in a later chapter. In the meantime, let us just call it mixing business with pleasure.

ASPIRATION

Another common one is the idea that a prime location with high quality improvements will always have appeal. That you cannot go wrong with up market property.

We see it all the time. People confuse desirability with performance.

In the property boom of the late eighties, luxury Sydney Harbour waterfront apartments were promoted as safe investments with unlimited growth potential. Located on one of the most beautiful harbours in the world they would always retain their value the market prophets said.

Homes on the harbour did attract the attention of the mega rich with record prices paid as a weekly occurrence. The growth in values was spectacular. Until it turned. Waterfront homes and apartments on the harbour that resold over the following years slumped in value by up to 50%.

No one will deny value growth of incredible proportions was achieved across the entire Sydney residential market in those years. But when the economy stalls and corporate profits turn down, executives no longer have the confidence to commit to large mortgages for home purchase if their future income potential is threatened. The very platform on which the luxury housing market stands is pulled away.

The top end of the market can be more volatile, has fewer participants and is more intricately linked to the economic and business cycles than other market segments.

The low to mid-range residential market is also dented at such times, but not as badly. Even the high-profile executives still must have a roof over their head, even if at a lower cost or lower rent. The mass market is not as dramatically affected as the top end. When the market peaks, values in the lower to mid-range still come down, but not as far. Where the luxury market slumped by up to 50% and in some isolated cases more, the mid-market reduced no more than 15%. Given that both markets over the preceding three years had increased by around 100%, which area do you suppose served the owners the best?

In every property cycle we consistently see investors purchase property that appeals to them personally, exposing them to unnecessary risk and ultimately less profit than that to which they are entitled. If they also purchase at the wrong time in the cycle that lower profit potential can fade away into losses and heartache.

EMOTION

Avoidance of emotional buying becomes a test of strength, coming from strong principles that should be set in concrete at the beginning of the property investment program.

The common property selection mistake is applying your personal views to what should be an objective process. The goal is to locate a property that the largest possible number of households in the area need, want, desire and can afford.

If you find yourself thinking "could I live in it?", you may have taken your eye of the ball.

Do not ask yourself if you could live in it, ask yourself who would live in it. The chances of you eventually occupying your purchase are remote.

Chapter 17

THE BIGGEST MISTAKE YOU CAN MAKE

The biggest mistake you can make in property, is not to own any investment real estate at all.

This is a statement we have used many times to make a powerful point. Technically though, it is untrue. The biggest, and most common mistake by far, would be buying at the peak of the market cycle and selling in the subsequent slump.

TRIGGERS

What causes someone to decide to invest in property?

Some people start thinking about property investment because they have paid off their home loan. Some decide to invest instead of buying a home. Others seek to minimise tax. Sometimes it is because friends or family are doing it.

Whatever the reason, it is what happens next that tends to trip people up.

Having made the decision to invest, the first thing many do is go straight to the market, searching real estate portals, making wish lists, making phone calls, and inspecting many properties at open houses on the weekends. They spend hours, and days and weeks, sometimes even months looking at property after property, never really knowing what they are looking for. It is not the answer.

To make it even tougher, many real estate agents do not have intimate knowledge of the principles of property investment.

THREE STEPS

There are three main steps you should take early in the property investment exercise. All essential elements in the process, and more importantly in getting the best possible results, mostly by avoiding mistakes.

The first is to be educated in the fundamental principles of property investment. To know how and why property investment works.

The second is to assess your financial position.

You need to know your borrowing capacity for investment purposes, as distinct from home ownership, as they are quite different.

You need to know the real after-tax cost of the investment. Some investors skip this step by assessing the rent, loan payments and estimated expenses, deducting one from the other and reaching a conclusion. As we have seen there are many hidden factors that such a calculation overlooks.

You need to know the real after-tax cost of the investment so you can ensure it fits your lifestyle. The reason you invest in the first place is to improve your lifestyle, not damage it. It helps to know what an investment will cost after taking everything into account.

The third and equally important final step is to get out into the real world and inspect properties. The learning curve in understanding the whole investment picture is best navigated by finding the properties that meet the investment criteria outlined in this book. It translates theory to the real world and makes it understandable.

These are the three essential tasks to be undertaken to have the complete picture - to be an informed property investor.

The biggest mistake you can make in property investment would most likely be caused by skipping any of these steps.

Chapter 18

FINDING THE PROPERTY

As we have already seen there are plenty of issues to address before looking for the property. You need to know how much you can afford to spend, how much you should borrow, as distinct from how much you can afford to borrow, the cost before and after tax and many other issues, all of which will help determine the property that will best suit your circumstances and meet your objectives.

Even after all the financial, taxation and market issues are addressed, there are still many things to consider and take into account. These are discussed in the chapter "Selecting the Best Property".

By way of context and example let us review some properties that we have assessed in the past as being among the better properties available for investment purposes at the time.

The following properties were recommended to our clients during the nineties and were included in the original version of this book as case studies. With the benefit of hindsight, we reprint them now with an update on how they have fared over the years since.

A WESTERN WATERFRONT

"The suburb of Chipping Norton is located just east of Liverpool, between Warwick Farm and Bankstown airport. It is the highest value, most up-market suburb in the south-west region of Sydney with median house prices in the suburb being around $280,000. It is bordered to the north by the Georges River.

During the 1980's the State of New South Wales and the Federal government initiated a bicentennial project to reclaim the Georges River, build parks and reserves and create sandy beaches. This created an environment which is unique in that part of Sydney of which many Sydneysiders would probably be unaware. We located property in Chipping Norton in a reasonable price range, which is effectively waterfront property in the heart of Sydney's south west.

It is aptly named "Lakeside" and comprises a complex of around two hundred home units with tennis courts, squash courts, swimming pools and intensively landscaped grounds. It is the only medium density complex in the suburb and little or no land exists in the area for further development of that type.

Two-bedroom home units at Lakeside were available from around $115,000 and when conducting the rental study for the project, we learned that rents being achieved were consistently around $200 per week and most tenants were middle managers and executives employed with companies based within a five-kilometre radius of the property. When we first discovered Lakeside, most of the project was held by a bank as mortgagee in possession, providing the opportunity to introduce many existing home units to our clients.

A question which arose whilst conducting the initial research, was the issue of proximity to public transport. Even though many might suggest that transport and tenants go hand in hand, our research suggested that at Lakeside this was not so. Being a suburb which is up-market for its region, residents tend to be the more affluent, higher income earners. This was confirmed by searching census data. It followed that a proportion of these people would have a need to rent, either because they were building a new home and had already sold the former home or were on secondment with their company from interstate for a year or two or had divorced and opted to rent for a period. People with reasonable incomes, who own cars and have somewhere to park at work, do not usually use public transport. This is the case in Chipping Norton.

When we checked the original construction dates of the various buildings in the project, we discovered that some of the buildings qualified for building depreciation allowance at a higher rate than the 2.5% which normally applies. This higher rate of 4% only applies to buildings which commenced construction between July 1985 and September 1987. It is not normally worth the effort to track down property built during this period because construction costs were significantly less than they are today and therefore there is less benefit, however in this case the construction cost had been unusually high due in part to the inclusion of extensive recreational facilities in the complex. Clients who purchased in those buildings will receive the benefit of that higher tax deduction for years to come.

The income a purchaser required, to borrow sufficient funds to purchase a home unit at Lakeside was around $32,000 gross income per year, clearly within reach of over half the working population. The net after tax holding cost, assuming a purchaser was on the highest marginal tax rate and borrowed 100% of the purchase price including all associated costs, was $42 per week. If values rose in a year at say 10% of the purchase price of $115,000, capital growth would equate to $11,500 weighed against an annual cost to hold the property of around $2,000. In time the holding cost will fall due to increasing rent while the growth will increase with compounding value. An excellent proposition".

Over twenty-five years later we have reviewed the price history of a sampling of apartments in this complex which reveals some interesting results in terms of price growth and exemplifies the behaviour of some property owners in relation to the property cycle.

Even though property data is a matter of public record, in deference to the current owners we have opted not to disclose specific apartment addresses although a diligent fact-checker will find these details in the records relatively easily. They are all located in Mead Drive, Chipping Norton.

Where an apartment has not sold recently, in order to establish an up-to-date price history, we have used the value estimated by Core Logic (a major property data company) as at January 2021.

Lakeside Apartment A

This apartment in the Lakeside complex is a typical two bedroom, one bathroom layout with single car garage and unrestricted resident access to the recreational facilities.

The original purchasers paid $118,000 and went on to sell the apartment nine years later in 2003 for $273,000, a gain of $155,000 or 9.77% per annum compound. An excellent result and presumably a happy experience for those investors.

The next people held it for four years and suffered a loss of over $60,000. A dramatically different result.

The difference is timing. If we look back at Sydney prices, in 1994 the market was just emerging from the downturn which followed the late eighties price boom. By late 2003 the market was close to a price peak.

The first purchasers bought in the early stages of recovery, sold near the peak and did well. The second owners bought at the market peak, sold in the subsequent slump, and lost money.

Keeping in mind it is not realistic to expect capital growth to continue at historical levels in a low inflation environment, if we calculate the growth rate from 1994 to the current estimated value, it works out to be 5.33% per annum compound. The inflation rate through the same period was 2.44% per annum leaving a real rate of increase of 2.89% per year. This is in line with our expectation that residential prices will increase over time at between 2% and 3% per annum above the rate of inflation.

YEAR	SALE PRICE
1994	$118,000
2003	$273,000
2007	$210,000
2021	$455,000

Lakeside Apartment B

A similar apartment to the previous example with a similar history. Again, the original purchasers did well, holding the property for nine years with a total gain of $140,000 or 9.25% per annum compound on purchase price. The second owners who bought as the market approached the price peak in 2003 also lost money but having held a little longer did not fare quite as poorly as their counterparts in Apartment A.

The growth rate over the life of the property is 5.24% per annum, inflation was 2.44% leaving a real rate of growth of 2.8% per annum.

Despite all sorts of anecdotal misinformation about why values may rise or fall, the lesson from these examples is that residential property is quite homogeneous in that similar properties will behave in similar ways – hence the importance of comparable sales data in residential valuation.

YEAR	SALE PRICE
1994	$115,000
2003	$255,000
2008	$230,000
2021	$445,000

Lakeside Apartment C

The third example in the Lakeside project is slightly different in being a three bedroom apartment, acquired a year later than the previous examples and with a more frequent sales history.

This apartment has had five owners over twenty-five years. All except one have done well in growth terms with each owner experiencing annual growth ranging from 6.0% to 6.5% a year. With inflation through that period of 2.45% a year, they achieved real growth rates of just over 3% per annum which is at the higher end of long-term expectations.

The people who bought the apartment in 2005 for $270,000 then sold in 2008 for $275,000 were the exception. They bought about eighteen months after the cyclical price peak. Prices were in decline and continued to bump along the bottom of the cycle for another three years. We can only speculate on their motive for selling three years after purchase, but we suspect, impatience due to lack of performance, may be the real reason. They did not lose much at face value, even after taking stamp duty and other costs into account, but the psychological damage may have been enormous. Will they ever invest in property again?

Together with the people in the other apartment examples who bought and sold during that 2003 to 2008 period, these are the people you meet who think property investment is a bad idea. Their timing was terrible, and they got their fingers burned.

YEAR	SALE PRICE
1995	$147,000
1999	$186,000
2005	$270,000
2008	$275,000
2018	$508,500
2021	$530,000

To all the pundits who say it is about time in the market, not timing the market, we disagree. It is about both.

There are optimum times to invest in residential property but there are clearly times when it is unwise. We refer you to the sales history of almost any property in Sydney, or any other market, as evidence.

As we have mentioned, three of the things that lead to property investment success are time, information, and patience. Another is always buy – never sell. Clearly life can get in the way, and people do choose to sell at various times for a variety of reasons. However, the people armed with the right information, who buy at the right time, resist the urge to sell and patiently accumulate property over the long term, get the best results and become the true advocates for residential property investment.

HIDDEN OPPORTUNITIES

'Hornsby is a major medium density area serving the upper north shore and northern districts of Sydney.

Around 1992 Hornsby Council rezoned a large area adjacent to the Hornsby CBD, to Residential (2C) zoning which allows three story walk-up home units to be constructed. The economy was in recession at the time and little new development occurred immediately following the rezoning. As the economy started to improve, and the market became more buoyant, developers and builders became more active.

Development applications started to appear at Council and a new wave of residential construction had begun. At first glance it seemed too much construction would occur. At the same time, we knew Hornsby to be a strong area. It is a nominated regional growth centre. There has been major activity in its central business district and more recently application has been made to Hornsby Council for massive redevelopment of the retail centre. It is the junction of two major rail lines and is a significant regional centre. It is also the only suburb on Sydney's upper north shore where there is a large medium density component within the mix of local housing. Being within reach of large employment centres Hornsby attracts tenants and home buyers.

Some expressed a view that so many new units would be built in the suburb due to the availability of zoned land that the market could be oversupplied and therefore prospects limited, even if only in the short term. Certainly, standing on any street corner in that area you could count at least half a dozen new buildings under construction. The impression was easy to understand. Some banks stopped lending in the area quoting potential oversupply as the reason.

We had doubts about the conventional wisdom and did some research. We calculated that the entire rezoned area would accommodate a specific number of home units. By making assumptions about the number that, when built, would be acquired by investors and placed in the rental market, we were able to determine that the new units would not meet the demand from population growth which had occurred in the area during the preceding years when very little new property was built.

We sourced a development of thirty two bedroom home units which could be acquired at around $210,000 each and which we estimated would rent at $235 per week. Local real estate agents at the time seemed to subscribe to the oversupply theory and informed us that around $210 would be the maximum achievable rent. By the time the building was completed, all the units had been acquired by our clients and we achieved rents of $245 per week on completion, reflecting a gross rental yield of 6.1%".

What had looked like a looming problem of oversupply played out to be more perception than reality. The building in Linda Street Hornsby proved very successful. We went on to recommend four projects in that rezoned area to investors during that brief window of opportunity.

All thirty apartments in the complex were originally purchased by people we advised at the time, some twenty-five years ago. With that insight, and now hindsight, we have reviewed the history of every apartment in the building. It reveals some interesting behaviour.

Firstly, of the thirty apartments, ten are still held by their original owners. We like to think these people are the always buy – never sell true believers, patiently practicing the art of long-term property investment.

Around 50% of the current residents in the complex are owner occupiers. This is in line with the ratio of owner occupiers to investors in most medium density properties. Even in a building where all original purchasers were investors and all residents were renting, as apartments have changed hands, the number of owner-occupiers has increased.

Of the twenty who have sold, the average holding period was eight years. The average growth rate they achieved was 4.78% per annum compound against an inflation rate of 2.45% leaving a real rate of growth of 2.33% in keeping with long term expectations.

All thirty apartments are similar in size and original finish. Purchase prices ranged from $203,000 to $217,900. An apartment purchased at the average price of $210,000 would be worth around $685,000 today.

The highest price paid in the building to date is $727,300 in April 2017, close to the market peak in July of that year. Prices have eased since. It was purchased by the original investor for $207,000.

Overall, the property has performed well, but the investors who sold did so at different points in the cycle so there have been substantial differences in the results they have achieved. Some did much better than others.

Nobody sold at less than they paid, although a couple came out behind in real terms. Both held the property for less than three years.

Of those who have sold, the strongest results saw five sellers achieve growth rates of around 6.5% per annum. All those people sold into the rising market between 2001 and 2003. That upturn ultimately peaked in early 2004. They had each held the property for seven to eight years.

These apartments were purchased during 1994 which we know was a low point in the Sydney residential price cycle. In that sense every investor in the building bought in the right market, at the right time. The difference in the results is totally attributable to whether they sold and when they sold.

We maintain the obvious winners are the people who have not sold. They have made solid gains in line with long term growth. They have not had to pay capital gains tax. They have not had to find a new home for the capital released from the property. They have not had to carry the transaction costs of moving capital around. Their investment is worth almost $700,000 and they are receiving over $24,000 a year in gross rent.

The five investors who sold after seven or eight years into the rising market also did extremely well. If you cannot or do not wish to hold long term, then buying low and selling high is the obvious objective. This is not easy. But just as it is better to buy too soon than too late, it is better to sell into a rising market than a falling one. The nearest any of the five most successful sellers got to the actual market peak in March 2004 was two of them sold just on a year prior, around March 2003.

Linda Street Hornsby - Apartment A

This is a typical two-bedroom, two-bathroom apartment. It has had four owners since new.

The original investor sold after eleven years making a price gain of 4.87% per annum or 2.42% real. All owners have done well with a slightly weaker result for the people who bought in 2005 just after the market peak in 2004. The gain over the life of the property based on the current value estimate of $685,000 is 4.7% per annum.

YEAR	SALE PRICE
1994	$207,000
2002	$325,000
2005	$330,000
2020	$675,000
2021	$665,000

Linda Street Hornsby - Apartment B

This is one of the apartments sold by the original investor into a firming market in 2002 generating an annual growth rate of 6.5%.

The purchaser in 2002 bought into a rising market which peaked around twenty months later. They sold three years later, experiencing a loss in real terms.

The people after them also did well. They paid $330,000 in 2005, held for fifteen years and sold for $675,000 in May 2020, right at the height of the pandemic, to show a growth rate of 4.94%.

YEAR	SALE PRICE
1994	$207,500
2005	$335,000
2009	$396,000
2015	$655,000
2021	$685,000

One of the lessons in these examples is that the real rate of return is what matters. It is surprisingly consistent, but even so it is not easy to think about growth rates in those terms. Nominal values are what we see day to day, and they are hard to ignore.

It does lay to rest some of the misconceptions about property values though. Property values are sometimes thought to double every seven years. That would translate into a growth rate of around 10% per annum. As we have seen, that is extremely unlikely in a low inflation environment.

People often refer to the property cycle as being about seven or eight years long. In Sydney, the price peaks have been in 1981, 1989, 2004 and 2017. The eighties cycle from peak to peak was eight years, however the two full cycles since have been significantly longer. The average is twelve years.

Another lesson may be the generally perceived state of a property market. The conventional wisdom can be, and often is, wrong.

People see construction happening and assume oversupply as they did in Hornsby.

More people buy property at the top of the market than at the bottom. That is how booms happen. From an investment perspective, most people buy property at the wrong time.

Crowd psychology is fascinating. There was a book published in 1841 titled "Extraordinary Popular Delusions and the Madness of Crowds" which documents examples of people getting swept up in market hysteria from Tulip mania to the South Sea bubble. We like to repeat the title to ourselves from time to time as a mantra to resist buying into frenzied markets.

But such frenzies are not only about people buying en masse at the wrong time. We think the very same people who buy at a high point in the price cycle tend to be the ones who give up and sell after only a few years, usually at the worst possible time. We saw a few examples in the previous sales histories. Getting swept up by market hype and buying at a high point is a judgement error - the greater mistake is to compound that error by deciding to sell within a few years, usually in the slump.

In finding the right property we need to be aware of the things that mask the real story and be prepared to do sufficient research to see past the conventional wisdoms and see the facts.

Chapter 19

RESORT PROPERTY

Much has been written about resort real estate. In previous books and newsletters, we have covered the subject in detail especially noting some of the dangers.

Buying property while on holidays has always been a no-no. Do not do it, we have warned with good reason. So often we have seen people take off to Queensland, or some other exotic place, and return the proud owner of an apartment.

IT CAN BE A DISASTER

Many may have done so, and the investment proved a worthwhile one. For many others it has been a disaster.

Even a few weeks in a location is insufficient time to carry out proper research to establish market value, market rent or any of the many factors that need to be considered before making a purchase. Nor does it give you the opportunity to consult with appropriate experts that you might normally rely on in your home environment.

THE TWO BEST EXAMPLES

Historically, real estate markets in resort areas have been comparatively weak. But that is changing. Many of the resort areas of past years have become major destinations for interstate migration. The best examples of this are the Gold Coast and the Sunshine Coast of Queensland. These two locations continue to attract more permanent residents. The Gold Coast is now the sixth largest urban area in Australia.

The solid growth in population has provided some strength to the real estate market in these areas which, when coupled with their domestic tourism appeal, make investment a more worthy proposition than it may have been in the past.

There has been a solid trend over the last few years of people moving from Sydney to regional parts of NSW, mostly to smaller cities and towns. Whilst that may provide some short-term strength in values in those locations the realities of the economic cycle remain a consideration.

During economic recessions and soft property markets, values in areas that are too tourism reliant may be heavily impacted. This could include ski-field chalets, wine-country cottages, or beachfront bungalows

A property market where a large proportion of the real estate is made up of second homes, or rental resort properties, softens quickly in any downturn.

If the economy is in recession, many owners in resort areas attempt to sell, dumping more property on a market where buyers are scarce so exacerbating the problem and prices slump further.

We are not painting a pretty picture here. Clearly investment in resort locations needs to be very cautiously considered.

This is why we refer to the Gold Coast and Sunshine Coast as two areas that have emerged as reasonable candidates. The Gold Coast has that rare combination of urbanisation and tourism that does make it unique.

TOURISM DEMAND - THE WILD CARD

The success of this type of venture will depend on many factors that are obvious, but the wild card is tourism demand, which can be volatile. Many people can justify this kind of investment by personal use during periods of low occupancy.

Although there are resort areas around Australia that have produced good incomes and growth over the years, they are few. The emotional draw of luxury real estate in exotic locations can be strong but, in most cases, should be resisted.

The Sunshine Coast whilst it is attracting more permanent residents has another unusual advantage in that residential development is being restricted by Local Government who wish to place a ceiling on population growth. It too has excellent tourism appeal.

While we place the Gold Coast on top of the list as a resort investment area, that does not mean it does not have its risks. It is still subject to the same demand supply pressures as any other property market. The investor should be wary of purchasing without a sound knowledge of the supply demand factors as well as the previously mentioned research that should be undertaken.

Notwithstanding these comments, the Gold Coast has matured as a strong growth area with an infrastructure that will help it to compete with the other major urban areas of Australia in the future.

There are several excellent resort locations within Australia that are worth consideration. But do not be emotionally motivated if you wish to make a sound choice. Apply all the tests first. It will be worth the effort for worry free ownership in the future.

Having said that, we often advocate the view it may be prudent to defer consideration of resort style property until a solid base of standard urban residential property has been established in a portfolio.

Chapter 20

STRESS-FREE PROPERTY MANAGEMENT

The way we go about our daily lives is changing fast. The way we bank, shop, invest, study, and even spend our leisure time, are all undergoing rapid change.

Thirty years ago, the proliferation of electronic funds transfer, the personal computer, mobile phones, instant information by phone, voice or digital device, social legislation, and many other developments, seemed a science fiction fantasy. In the business of property investment management and ownership the changes have also been substantial.

Property market data and information is available from statutory authorities at the push of a button, rental payments can be made by bank or electronic transfer, and legislative changes in areas such as capital gains tax, Rental Tribunal, and property related Anti-Discrimination issues are happening with increasing frequency.

KEEPING UP WITH CHANGE

Residential property remains the most attractive form of investment available, however as in all aspects of life, the rules are constantly changing, and special care is required to ensure your investment serves you well into the future.

Whilst the benefits of sophisticated technology are many, it also means the business of owning rental property is becoming more and more complicated. A specialised knowledge of property investment, property law, banking and finance, investment analysis and many other related skills are required to maximise returns, and successfully manage investment property.

The day-to-day management of your property is an important activity in the investment process and starts with people. Whether you choose to use a local real estate agency or a larger specialist management company, the quality and experience of their people makes the difference.

The days of real estate agencies using their young, inexperienced receptionist as a part time property manager are over.

SELECTING THE RIGHT TENANT

The selection of a good tenant requires attention to detail, research, knowledge of property law as well as compassion and people skills.

Property managers understand that a vacant property is non-productive. Despite this, it may be prudent for a property to be vacant for a few extra days whilst the right tenant is found, rather than leasing a property to a tenant who may cause problems in the future at potentially greater cost.

For this reason, owners who list their property to let with several agents, may be doing themselves a disservice. In the race to be the first to find a tenant and receive a one-off casual letting fee, some agents may lower their selection criteria or skip steps in the process. This is especially so if that agent is not responsible for the ongoing management.

There are four main things to check to assess the suitability of a prospective tenant:

Employment - Stable employment and regular income helps to ensure rent is paid and paid on time.

- **Income** - The amount of income determines the affordability of rent. We have always applied an income test which is akin to bank loan assessment criteria. If the gross rent exceeds about 35% of the prospective tenant's household income problems may emerge.

- **Rental history** - Checks on previous tenancies help establish a stable rental history. When someone applies for a new tenancy, the property manager will usually request copies of the applicant's rental ledgers from their previous managing agent. This shows the amount and frequency of all payments made by the tenant during their previous lease.

- **References** - Bank and other references may indicate reliability. Legislation regarding credit reference checks prevent real estate agents from using the mainstream credit rating agencies to establish credit worthiness of prospective tenants. This makes it essential that every alternative reference source available is checked to determine the background and reliability of a prospective tenant.

There are three main tenant databases in Australia. They are operated by private companies and are effectively blacklists of people who have left rental properties in the past with arrears or debts which exceed the rental bond or have been involved in malicious damage. The criteria to be listed varies from state to state. These online databases are updated by property managers throughout the country who subscribe to the service.

These checks and reference services have been controversial in the past as they deal with sensitive, personal information, however they are relevant and important. If someone borrows the money to buy a property, the lender seeks to know as much about them as possible to assess the risk. If they apply to rent a property, they are also committing to a large financial obligation and occupation of a major financial asset. Not a big difference.

Changes to anti-discrimination legislation specifically relating to rental property also requires careful management to avoid later conflict in our increasingly litigious society.

PROPERTY INSPECTIONS

Once a new lease agreement commences, the property is immediately inspected specifically noting cleanliness and condition. Each inspection undertaken follows an inspection check list, paying special attention to details of additional fixtures and appliances that may be included with the property. Attention to detail at this time can minimise the possibility of disputes in the future.

When tenants vacate, the property is carefully inspected again. Upon vacating, it is reasonable to expect the property be thoroughly cleaned and in similar condition to the commencement of the lease agreement although the tenant is not liable for fair wear and tear.

Regular inspections are conducted usually every six months to check the cleanliness and state of repair of the property. This information is then submitted to owners, in written report form, often with photos.

These formal inspections afford owners the opportunity of checking the condition of their property and ensures that any damage has been reported and repaired promptly. If market conditions necessitate a rent review upon lease expiry, it makes good sense to inspect the property before formulating an opinion of the new market rent. The object of maintenance is to preserve the capital asset and maximise rental income.

MAINTENANCE AND DAMAGE CONTROL

The object of maintenance is to preserve your capital asset. In addition, effective management and maintenance procedures will:

- Maintain an appealing appearance and therefore the marketability of the property.
- Prevent tenant dissatisfaction or complaint which can cause tenants to withhold rent.
- Reduce the vacancy factor.
- Increase income and capital growth for the owner.

Some property owners believe spending money on repairs and maintenance does not benefit the net return on their property. Eventually when they wish to re-let their property, they may find that the premises have become run down, which in turn affects the quality of tenant the property attracts, the gross rent achieved and ultimately the net return on their investment.

There are significant legislative requirements that must be complied with at all times.

Managing property maintenance requires careful balance to ensure the property remains attractive to the market whilst maximising net returns and complying with all relevant legislation.

AVOIDING BAD DEBTS

Although unpaid rent money may be retrievable from bonds held with the Rental Bond Board, our policy has always been one of "prevention is better than cure". Naturally, we would prefer to avoid bad debts altogether. Having the best possible tenant is much easier than recovering bad debts, and this is why we consider tenant selection criteria to be so important. Maintaining a healthy, business-like relationship with tenants helps in resolving any problems before they become a disruptive dispute.

The collection of rent when due, and prompt and regular accounting to property owners is the primary responsibility of a property manager. To control rent arrears, it is important to have a well maintained, well understood, easy to use rental payment system.

Tenants may be offered the option of paying their rent direct into the property manager's trust account by deposit at any Bank branch or by electronic transfer from their bank account. These methods of rent collection have proven very effective in minimising late or non-payment of rent. Most tenants elect to remit rent by bank deposit and a significant number authorise automatic recurring payments direct from their bank account.

The days of a tenant going to a shop-front real estate office on a Saturday morning to pay the rent in cash are long gone. Most agents will not accept cash at all.

Firm follow up of late payments is essential in preventing the escalation of bad debts.

Most property managers use a direct banking system to remit monthly rents to owners. This is done via electronic funds transfer, and ensures funds are cleared quickly, and reach owners accounts the day they are processed.

TENANT DISPUTES

In New South Wales the Residential Tenancies Tribunal has been constituted as a specialist Tribunal to determine all matters relating to residential property. It's main jurisdiction and powers include:

- To make orders for the payment of unpaid rent, debt or damages;
- Order the performance of work.
- Orders for the termination of residential tenancy agreements and for possession of property;
- Orders in respect of breaches or disputes relating to Residential Tenancy Agreements -including orders requiring action in performance of the agreement or for compensation etc, even if in the nature of an injunction or specific performance, and in circumstances when that remedy would be unavailable under the general law;

- Orders relating to rental bonds, taking the jurisdiction of the Consumer Claims Tribunal.

Other powers include:

- Order that the landlord or any other person may enter the premises;
- Authorise the landlord or tenant to alter, remove, or add locks for security;
- Order that a rent increase is excessive, and make an interim order suspending payment of the whole or part of the rental increase;
- Order compensation from the tenant to the landlord if the tenant fails to comply with an order for possession;
- Declare the premises have been abandoned;
- Order compensation by the tenant for loss caused to the landlord by abandoning the property.

Except in unusual circumstances lawyers are not permitted to represent the parties in Tribunal matters.

A LONG TERM RELATIONSHIP

Many issues which are not day-to-day property management tasks may arise during the course of ownership of investment property. Some of these are covered in the following sections.

Building a long-term relationship with property managers who have a well-rounded experience in all facets of the investment process can have many advantages.

Your property manager should be more than a collector of rent and supervisor of maintenance. They should also be informed advisers in all aspects of finance and taxation as they relate to property or at least have ready access to expertise in those areas.

TAXATION & FINANCE

Over recent years several significant changes have been made to the taxation treatment of returns from residential investment property. These changes have been discussed in other chapters of this book but suffice to say that property management staff must be watchful in this area. For example, expenditure on replacement items such as carpets, blinds, light fittings, furniture, or appliances are often overlooked as claimable depreciation items.

CAPITAL GAINS TAX

It is important to maintain detailed records of capital expenditures, acquisition and disposal costs, changes in beneficial ownership and changes of use or occupation for future Capital Gains Tax calculations.

GROUP TAX ADJUSTMENT

Many investors hold negatively geared property on which they are subsidising the investment by amounts which may have a short term negative effect on their lifestyle even though a tax refund is received after the end of the financial year.

As we discussed earlier, an application can be lodged with the Tax Office whereby group tax instalments are reduced through the year by an amount equivalent to the estimated tax credit or refund which would otherwise be received up to eighteen months later. The result is a smoother cash flow and avoids lending money to government interest free at the expense of a comfortable lifestyle.

A good property manager will be able to provide much of the information required to complete the application.

FINANCIAL POSITION & ACCUMULATION

A common question from investors involves knowing when the time has arrived to consider further investment in property as a result of increased equity in currently owned properties. When to roll the snowball and move down the path followed by James and Susan in our earlier examples.

Periodically reviewing the overall position of your property investments is a prudent action. Some investors revise their asset and liability statement as frequently as monthly. Others seek to review their property portfolio on an annual basis. Either way your property manager can help with this by providing value updates as required.

As an owner you naturally retain a responsibility to manage the manager. The appointment of the right property manager is essential and should become a long-term relationship of mutual benefit. Ownership of rental property can be an enjoyable and rewarding experience.

Regular contact between manager and owner is important and should be initiated by both parties. Good communication will alleviate problems that arise out of misunderstandings and lack of suitable explanations and or instructions.

Many strategies can be implemented to deal with market conditions to minimise vacancies and maximising income. These should be initiated by your manager but consultation between both parties is helpful in putting such plans into operation.

If you currently own rental investment property and you are not satisfied with the service you are receiving you have two choices; one is to bring your manager up to standard the other is to change managers.

It may not be entirely your managing agent's fault. Perhaps you have not properly instructed them about maintenance policy or tenant criteria. You may be difficult to contact for consultation. Some owners have even been known to demand top service for a reduced fee.

Nevertheless, sometimes a change in management is warranted. Do not hesitate if you conclude you are not receiving the standard of service to which you are entitled.

It need not be a difficult or embarrassing task. Select a new manager carefully, preferably by personal interview. Meet the staff involved and question them on expertise, policy, and results. Inspect sample stationery including rent statements, pro forma letters, previous advertising copy and most importantly ask for references from other clients. If you are not completely happy, move on. It is your property and income at risk.

When you have selected a suitable new manager just give them the written authority to assume management and they will pick up files, and keys from the former agent without you having to make any contact with your old manager in any way at all.

FEES

We expect a great deal from property managers. In New South Wales, most charge management fees of between 5% and 8% including GST. There may also be charges for other specific services such as letting fees, maintenance supervision or tribunal attendance.

Property management is a labour-intensive business. The property management department in a typical real estate agency rarely makes super profits. But to the agency, it represents regular cash flow, a store of capital and a source of future sales listings.

When you find a property manager who will negotiate their management fee down to the lower half of the range, it is likely they are not profitable. If that is the case, they are either subsidising the business or heavily cutting corners on resources, including people.

It may also be that their management fee is low, but all other fees are high. They will supply you with a schedule of their fees and it should be obvious if that is the case.

The fees you pay property managers are fully tax deductible.

Overall, we think the best approach to property management fees is this. They work for you. Expect excellent service and value that service. But be prepared to pay for it. It is worth it.

THE MANAGEMENT AGENCY AGREEMENT

When you enter into the management agreement there will be a termination clause. This requires you to give the agent a period of notice to end the agreement. It has become common for agents to seek the longest possible period with up ninety days' notice required in some cases.

Whilst you may be happy to pay their full fee and expect excellent service, if that service is not forthcoming, being able to readily replace them is important. It keeps them on their toes and you in control. Fourteen days' notice is plenty but thirty is probably reasonable.

Chapter 21

FUTURE TRENDS IN PROPERTY

Much of this book focuses on the experience and lessons of the past, to understand and predict the future. But there will always be trends, developments and changes that are relatively unique to a particular era, and this is especially true of the changing needs of the community for different types of, and uses, for property.

In an earlier book, published by Fred in 1969 titled "How to Get Real Estate Rich", a number of predictions were made on the types of property which would emerge over following years. Remember these predictions were made over fifty years ago. At that time none of them were apparent and none existed.

The following is an extract:

> *"...there will be new opportunities not yet dreamed of.*
>
> *When the cities of Australia establish expressway systems and improve major national highways, new opportunities will open up for investments in abundance.*
>
> *New roads will allow the mass of the population to move faster to new places and locations for apartments and shopping centres, so housing communities will be found at the extremity of the super highways, bringing extraordinary capital growth to areas now considered "too far out".*

There will be a food revolution in the country in the next ten years. Restaurants, drive-in restaurants, food bars and supermarkets will change radically in concept, design and location.

Food service centres will span superhighways with special access ramps so as not to disturb the flow of traffic. Supermarkets will be built on 50-acre lots, free standing without other stores, just surrounded by huge parking areas. Restaurants will give off-street parking and car service. Drive-in food bars of modern design and attractive architecture will be built and designed on major roads and in shopping centres.

The Regional Centre will be bigger and contain many more community activities, but more important, it will be located further out of town to service the new, expanding populations, bringing with it increased activity and increased land values.

Large scale residential communities will develop on the fringe of cities, creating a new way of life for home-owners and tenants.

These developments will contain private clubs for residents that incorporate a community lounge room, card room, party rooms, bars, billiard room, gymnasiums, health spa, and sauna rooms.

With these developments there will be golf courses, putting greens, tennis courts, swimming pools, children's playing areas, pre-school kindergartens, child-minding centres, bowling greens, and many more features for community use, all for the benefit and happiness of the occupants.

While such development is taking place on the extremities of the expressways, the city will continue to rise upwards. There is no way that we can prevent the heart of a city from building up because there is no other way to go.

Office buildings will take over downtown areas as retail shopping becomes almost non-existent, but office buildings will be taller, have more open space around them and include tenant facilities such as conference rooms, restaurants, ample parking, swimming pools, games rooms and libraries.

Industrial parks will become the development of the future in this field. There will be planned industrial centres offering open space and park lands surrounding industrial facilities, perhaps underground, parks and recreation facilities to occupy extra daylight hours as working periods decrease".

Resort development will also help shape the future, as it always does in a country where the work force is constantly earning more money in less time and retiring at younger ages, with large superannuation cheques - especially in a country like Australia, that has such beautiful coastline and mountain resort areas."

Just as so much of that predicted fifty years ago is now accepted as standard, when we first published The Wealth Power of Property almost twenty-five years ago, we made a further round of comments about the future of property.

TECHNOLOGY

"Australia has one of the highest penetrations of new technology on the planet. Mobile phones, video cassette recorders and personal computers are examples of new technologies we have embraced with vigour, causing a remarkably high percentage of households, in world terms, to acquire these items. In marketing jargon, we would be labelled "early adopters". We like our toys.

In property terms, the effect of these technologies is two-fold. Firstly, we must keep them somewhere. It is rare these days to walk into an Australian home and not find a desk with a computer and other related equipment. Most often the desk is in a spare bedroom.

No doubt, at some future point these technologies will become smaller, or be built into the property itself, but in the meantime, they must be accommodated, and they take up space. We can see this having an impact on smaller, old style properties, in particular, studio and one bedroom dwellings which are, to some extent, either becoming redundant, or at best, and being mindful of the large number being constructed in CBD areas, do not encourage long term occupation due to their increasingly limited use.

The other impact of technology on property is the long awaited and much talked about ability to live further from densely populated areas, and "telecommute". That is, to move further from the city, with its pollution, traffic, crime, and other perceived drawbacks, to live in a quieter location, to gain a lifestyle advantage.

In the United States, where this trend is gathering momentum, satellite towns around large cities are rapidly developing where a significant proportion of residents may commute by normal means to the city a couple of days each week and base their work at home the balance of the time, using various communication technologies to remain in contact.

This trend has been labelled "Penturbian" development, or the fifth wave of urban development. It has also been explained as a reversal of the industrial revolution, whereby, large factories replaced cottage industries, and concentrated populations into relatively small areas, close to employment. Penturbian development has the opposite effect, allowing people to live further afield and continue to earn a living.

To some extent it still sounds a little like science fiction, but the fact that banks, and other employers are now setting up large numbers of their employees this way, tends to suggest it is real, and we are seeing the beginnings of a major trend. It may take a generation to fully develop, but one can only conclude outlying areas around major cities will benefit over the years ahead."

For most of the last twenty-five years we have not recommended investment in one bedroom or studio apartments as they did become impractical and more the domain of transient occupants such as inner-city domestic and international students. There was even a period when banks were reluctant to lend on that type of property.

As we know, the shrinking of digital devices did happen and these days we are much more comfortable with one-bedroom apartments, although we prefer them to be a little more generous in size than in the past with a minimum of 65 square metres in internal floor-space. We are still not keen on studio or bed-sitter style apartments.

The incidence of people working from home has been a growing trend over the last couple of decades but has taken a giant leap forward with the pandemic. This will clearly hasten the movement of people away from densely populated areas to lifestyle-oriented, sea-change and tree-change locations. It will also benefit the outer areas of major cities.

ELECTRONIC SHOPPING

> *"Electronic banking and electronic shopping will affect our future living habits and more particularly, impact retail and commercial property.*
>
> *Shopping by computer and telephone in whatever its future form, will mean that retailers, especially food, will no longer need such large retail premises and may not need to locate in prime retail centres at all.*
>
> *It is interesting to note how many of the large retail chains have sold their real estate in favour of becoming tenants. No one could argue that their money could be better invested in their core business activity, that of retailing, but could they also have an eye on the future growth prospects of the real estate? They may not in future need to locate in such high rent property. Could their thinking be, better someone else own it than them?*
>
> *The banks, who are already well down the track in off-loading their branch premises, are actively discouraging customers from physically going to the bank."*

We have all noticed the changes to retailing over the last twenty-five years. Record stores and bookstores are almost extinct having been replaced in most shopping malls by nail, hair, and massage salons – the personal services that are not available online.

Food and other retailers continue to have a bricks and mortar presence but as we know their online sales continue to grow and will eventually overtake instore sales.

Banks continue to operate branches although they have shifted in purpose from transaction processing to a store selling financial products. The number of branches has fallen dramatically.

We thought one of the casualties would be travel agents, yet somehow their numbers seemed to increase or at least remain the same over the last couple of decades. There is evidence in the last five years that their numbers are shrinking. And that was before the pandemic stopped international travel in its tracks.

In many areas, at least until the pandemic arrived, it was starting to feel as if shopping centres were almost exclusively comprised of supermarkets, travel agencies, clothing boutiques, sushi-train restaurants, and personal care services.

Remember the old economic wisdom that the basic needs in life are food, clothing, and shelter? Not a bad thing to remember when thinking about investment.

FUTURE PLANNED COMMUNITIES

"We have discussed the possibility of home-based work centres allowing more people to telecommute from fringe areas. In the future this will give rise to new satellite towns, master planned to create improved lifestyles.

The Gold Coast in Queensland has seen what is up to now a poor attempt to create this kind of environment. Unfortunately, to date it has been directed more towards the investor (and the rental market), than the owner-occupier, but that will change, and is changing. The best examples are communities like Sanctuary Cove, Hope Island, Arundel Hills, and Palm Meadow. These are the forerunners.

There will be more, and they will continue to keep pace with the times, providing the services such communities will need. Even now they provide country clubs, food services, retail shopping, recreational clubs and spas, golf courses, tennis courts, pools, in-house movies, cable television and organised community activities. Future planned communities like these will be in strong demand and should, in the main, be successful enterprises and create fine lifestyles for their residents.

Retirement villages have improved markedly since their inception, but they still have a long way to go. Our aging population will provide a burgeoning market and will demand additional facilities. Lower densities should be foremost. However, many of the features of design and comfort we have outlined in respect of other market segments will also apply to retirement housing".

A large segment of the market for master-planned communities is clearly the baby boomers. Boomers are now sixty to seventy-five years old. In the last ten years alone, the number of people aged over sixty-five has increased from 13% to 16% of the population. The groundswell of demand these people represent is substantial and we are still only in the early stages of the impact they will have on housing over the next twenty years.

Retirement living is evolving, but slowly. The retirement village model will change in response to growing demand over the next couple of decades. The re-branding of the "old age home" with the concept of "independent living communities" is more than just changing labels. We do not think the teenagers of the sixties and seventies will settle for cheese sandwiches and bingo in their later years.

We see the possibility of multiple occupancy landholdings becoming more prevalent. These communities will further develop ideas like self-sufficient power generation, community vegetable gardens, art co-operatives and other shared resources.

CITY LIVING

As Fred said in 1969;

> *"the central business districts of Australia will continue to build upwards and continue to squeeze retail outwards to the suburbs and satellite districts.*
>
> *To those who have said over the years that our cities will transform into more residential oriented communities, we have always, and still do, predict that they will not. We gave our reasons earlier in this chapter for why population movements will be more outwards than inwards, and this trend will have an influence on the ability of downtown and inner-city locations to attract permanent, as distinct from transient, residents."*

Fifty years later, retail stores have moved away from the CBD district into the suburbs, and the overall trend in population movement continues to be away from inner areas. The much-touted café society of the inner city idea does appeal to small segments of the market but is not a significant growth trend.

THE FUTURE

The future is always exciting with the promise of new technologies, medical breakthroughs and even new ways of thinking in how we interact with each other and behave as a community.

Driverless cars, drone deliveries, virtual medical services, legalised marijuana, contactless payment systems, artificial intelligence and wearable devices that replace smartphones are either already appearing or are barrelling down on us like a Mack truck.

There is speculation that political and economic systems will morph and adapt over the period ahead. Certainly, the extreme income inequality that is evident in many western countries cannot go on forever. It is just not mathematically possible, let alone desirable.

Eventually we will all vote for our political representatives electronically. Some think we will also vote on specific issues during parliamentary terms.

In terms of understanding current and future trends, demographic shifts and even the impact of the pandemic, the good news is the next Australian Census, which only occurs every five years, will take place across the country in August 2021. The results will be fascinating.

Some people think we will all return to business as usual once the pandemic subsides, and that may happen, but we find ourselves hoping the new normal is different.

We hope people are increasingly able to work remotely and spend more time with friends and family. We hope the environment benefits from a gentler pace of life. We hope people find a new appreciation for community.

We hope, despite the dramatic impact it has had on everyone, this pandemic will be seen in hindsight as a positive turning point. But as always, no matter what happens, people will still need to live somewhere, and residential property markets will roll on into the future providing enormous opportunity for the informed investor.

EPILOGUE

When we first published The Wealth Power of Property, we were actively involved in the business of advising clients on property and property markets, seeking out superior property investments for those clients and providing property management services for the properties we recommended. That is no longer the case.

Fred is now 86 years old and long retired. He lives on the northern beaches of Sydney overlooking the Pittwater waterway. He still owns multiple investment properties but has reduced the size of his portfolio over the last ten years. He is thinking about buying a new boat.

Brett is in his sixties and is semi-retired. He lives on the Pittwater waterfront in Sydney's northern beaches. He continues to write about property, plays bass guitar in local bands, grows vegetables in the backyard, and spends time and money on a houseboat called Clementine.

While we do not spend our days meeting with investors, we do have industry people submitting properties to us and occasionally we see stand-out propositions which we are happy to share with you.

Leave your details at www.therealestateanalyst.com and we will let you know when the better good ones appear.

We wish you good fortune and many years of successful residential property investment.

Keep in touch and let us know how you prosper in the future. We hope that fifteen years from now or even earlier you join the long and growing list of residential property multi-millionaires.

It is still a good life!

Printed in Dunstable, United Kingdom

91218878R00100